MISSION

Books by Roger G. Kennedy

ROGER G. KENNEDY

MISSION

THE HISTORY AND ARCHITECTURE OF
THE MISSIONS OF NORTH AMERICA

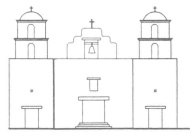

EDITED AND DESIGNED BY DAVID LARKIN

Photography by Michael Freeman

A MARC JAFFE BOOK

Houghton Mifflin Company

BOSTON   NEW YORK   1993

For information about permission to reproduce selections from this book, write to Permissions, Houghton Mifflin Company, 215 Park Avenue South, New York, New York 10003.

Library of Congress Cataloging-in-Publication Data

Kennedy, Roger G.
    Mission : the history and architecture of the missions of North America / Roger Kennedy ; edited and designed by David Larkin ; photography by Michael Freeman.
        p.   cm.
    "A Marc Jaffe book."
    Includes bibliographical references and index.
    ISBN 0-395-63416-4
    1. Spanish mission buildings — United States.
2. Architecture, Spanish colonial — United States.
I. Larkin, David.   II. Title.
NA707.K39   1993
726'.5'0973 — dc20   93-3809
                                                                      CIP

Printed in Italy
by Sfera/Garzanti – Milano

SFE   10 9 8 7 6 5 4 3 2 1

The drawings on pages 228–231, together with their annotations and glossary, are reproduced by permission of the Southwest Parks and Monuments Association, Tucson, Arizona.

The photographs are by Michael Freeman except for those on the following pages:
Robert Frerck/Odyssey, 32, 35, 40, 42–43, 52, 55, 57, 58, 59, 63, 68, 73, 74
George H. H. Huey, 7, 13, 15, 142, 162, 163, 164, 165, 167, 168
Roger G. Kennedy, 91
Jack Kotz, 100–101, 102, 187, 188, 189
David Messick, 176, 202, 203, 212, 213
John Ruebartsch, 90, 233
Stephen Trimble, 140, 145
American Museum of Natural History, illustration, 108; photograph, 110
Arthur Shilstone, National Geographic Society, illustration, 29

To Ruth and Rob

CONTENTS

Come to it slowly.
It is not so empty as it seems.

Come quietly and listen:
Beneath the wind there are other voices.

Nuestra Señora de los Angeles de Porciuncula de los Pecos,
New Mexico.

Come quietly and tread with care:
Beneath the wind drift and rubble there are other rooms.

Touch. Run your hands along the arches shaped like those on the shores of the Tigris and Euphrates.

The Greeks did build churches using arches, but the Romans marked the edges of their world with them.
At Pecos arches marked the edge of the evangelism of the Roman church.

Red is the color of the church and convento, of the school and workrooms, the red of Rome. Red stands beside and within the gray walls of the ancient ones who thronged this hillside and farmed these fields, long before the coming of an arch or a horse or a sword or a cross.

THE FRIARS WENT FORTH from Catholic Europe to gain converts among the American Indians. Though many of the missionaries were not Spaniards, they had another task: to colonize America for Spain and thereafter to deny its riches to any other power.

INTRODUCTION

THE FIRST FRANCISCAN FRIARS came into Mexico in 1524 in the bloody footsteps of the conquistador Hernán Cortés. There were twelve of them. This number was probably no accident; the Roman Catholic Church was starting anew. After these Twelve Apostles came many more, and within five decades nearly four hundred missions were constructed in central Mexico, in the most formidable building campaign within so brief a time in the history of Christendom.

Catholic Europe arrived in Mexico together with imperial Spain, and only a little more than a century after the Aztecs cleared the way. The Aztec contribution to the success of Spain, as distinguished from the mission of Catholicism, was in showing how a military elite might supervene upon the masses. All that was required of Cortés was that he survive long enough to substitute himself for the emperor of the Aztecs, and put a Spanish elite in the place of the Aztec.

Furthermore, the behavior of the Aztecs, prior to their brief spasm of competition with the Spaniards, had created such hostility to their rule that the Europeans found ready allies. It must be said, however, that Cortés and his Indian allies, who were far more numerous than his own force, barely prevailed.

Immediately thereafter, many of those who had transferred their fealty to Spain converted to Catholicism. After many Indians who had resisted the foreigners were wiped out by European and African diseases, and after commensurate losses were suffered by those who were already acquiescent, it became obvious that European diseases were an identifiable source of suffering, while European religion asserted itself to be a means of redemption. Indian resistance to Catholicism increased, but the mission continued in the face of both political and religious counterattacks.

Beyond the first vineyard of the faith shimmered deserts and mountains requiring even greater exertion and promising much less satisfaction. Nonetheless, scores of new missions were embedded in the oases and green widenings of the river systems among the forbidding dry mountains of northern Mexico.

The cost was high. The energy of Catholic Europe was already flagging when the Jesuits came into Baja California and Arizona, and the Franciscans into New Mexico and Texas. The friars moved onward, impelled by genuine religious zeal. Some of their military escorts shared that zeal, but in addition they were drawn by glints of precious metals among the rocks and in the jewelry worn by the Indians. All the while, the commanders of the military were being enjoined by Madrid to occupy advance posts in which they might resist attacks by either Europeans or Indians.

By the middle of the sixteenth century, Spain feared intrusion by France and Britain upon its sources of precious metals in central and northern Mexico. As the eighteenth century unfolded, Spanish apprehensions were increased by the growing power of the Russian Empire and of the United States.

In Florida, where Jesuits and the mendicant orders often labored simultaneously, more than forty missions and asistencias were established. This effort extended from the Mission Ajacan on Chesapeake Bay, to San Miguel in South Carolina, across Georgia to Santa Cruz de Nanipacha in central Alabama, and down to the Gulf Coast. None of these missions survived into the nineteenth century, even though Spain held Florida until 1821. Official political history shows few interruptions in Spanish control over three hundred years, but there were very few Spaniards in Florida at any time, and their hand was scarcely felt in the interior.

The forty missions established in New Mexico and the dozen or so in Arizona fared somewhat better, for there the Spanish presence was more dense and isolated from competition with other Europeans. The fervency of the missionary friars is eloquently demonstrated in archaeology, for the ruins of churches that were laid out first are often the largest. As time went on, the mission effort was characterized by retrenchment, followed, in some notable cases, by abandonment.

The slow decline of the missions were marked not only in the diminishing size of foundations nesting one inside another but in the dispiriting sequence of statistics reported to Mexico City. Epidemics swept away many parishioners. The Indians noted the failure of the friars' incantations to protect them, and defected. Marauding Apache and Navajo made off with cattle, sheep, and slaves, while Spanish soldiers, always too few, attempted to defend them, often too late. As the droughts of the 1660s and 1670s afflicted the remaining villagers, many of them may have taken the failure of crops to be a final sign that they could expect little of practical use from the new religion. Some of the most architecturally ambitious missions (such as those southeast of Albuquerque) were abandoned by the close of the 1670s.

Disease, marauders, and drought would have been present even if all governors had been wise, all soldiers considerate, and all friars saintly, and if none of these had bickered with each other. The truth was otherwise, and when the Pueblo Indians in 1680 coordinated into a general rising what had previously been a series of less comprehensive defections, the entire district, from the western pueblos of the Zuñi and Hopi to Pecos, went up in smoke. In Arizona the largest of a series of Pima wars was barely won by the Spaniards in the 1750s. In New Mexico in 1680, the Pueblos drove out the soldiers and missionaries. Before they could return with any hope of remaining, they had to reach agreement with the Pueblos on two matters of common interest.

First, the two groups worked out their relationship with each other. Governance of the Indian communities was left almost entirely in Indian hands. Their religious observances were no longer subjected to repression; to this day each new parish priest must sort out his own ways of accommodating Indian preferences and those of the pope. Many Indians took Spanish surnames and participated in Christian observances as well. The Hopi of Arizona remained beyond this rapprochement. Their experience had been especially bitter under Spanish rule, and they were sufficiently isolated as to constitute a strategic problem beyond the reach of Spanish force. Having burned out one of the most impressive of the missions in their territory, at Awatovi, they were never remissionized.

Second, the Pueblos and Spaniards entered into a military alliance against the Apache and Navajo, who were gaining strength and had achieved skill in cavalry tactics. Horses were now running wild on the plains and could be taken by skillful riders. Gunpowder and weapons could be obtained at first, second, or third hand from the French.

Many missions were put back into service or rebuilt, some, such as that at Pecos, on a considerably smaller scale. After all this turmoil, the landscape of New Mexico was left with the nation's most comprehensive collection of picturesque ruins in European styles.

In Texas the two Spanish advances produced a total of thirty-four missions. It was not just the depredations of the French, Apache, and Comanche that brought this number down to a handful by 1820 or 1821. The Indians of Texas, unlike the Pueblos, were not accustomed to living closely together over centuries in the same place. They did not find common interest with the Spaniards in the deployment of soldiers and firearms to stand off other Indians or other Europeans. Lacking the resistance to urban diseases that saved some New Mexican and Arizonan villagers, they died in large numbers when brought into compounds. Few of the survivors found an incentive to continue to stay in such places, so the mission population diminished to the vanishing point. San Antonio de Valero (the Alamo) was inventoried and disbanded in 1793; only 38 parishioners were left at La Purísima Concepción, about 130 at San José, and another 70 or so elsewhere in the San Antonio complex. The last of the Texas missions, founded in 1791, was Refugio, where the San Antonio River wanders into the Gulf of Mexico; the Refugio mission struggled along unheeded until it was finally auctioned off in 1829, the last to go.

The handsomely restored group of mission buildings around San Antonio recalls the brevity and courage — the foolishness, some might say — of the Texas missionary endeavor. The Indians, after experimenting with the friars' modes of addressing the forces of nature that determined survival, were not universally impressed with the results. If salvation meant starvation, they showed little desire to be saved. They found many occasions to make off with the horses, cattle, and sheep that the army left unrequisitioned. Yet the friars kept on trying.

The rise and decline of the California missions came later than the Texas adventure. After some seaborne probes in search of port facilities, slaves, and fruit, Spanish penetration of the coastal plain got under way in the 1770s. Most construction occurred in the first twenty years of the nineteenth century in a brief, intense, late, and embattled flowering of the missionary impulse.

Like the nations of Texas, the California Indians, though a remarkably heterogenous group, included no urban, drilled, and docile societies like those that took to Spanish rule in Mexico, nor were they villagers threatened by nomad attacks, such as the Pueblo people of New Mexico. From the prosperous and artistic coastal Chumash to the desert tribes barely subsisting in the Mojave Desert, they had lived without large towns, and on their own terms. They did not adapt happily to the regimentation of the missions. Spanish archives record Indian "uprisings" in 1771, 1775, 1776, 1805, 1817, 1824, 1826, 1829, and 1832, the year in which the Mexican government secularized the missions, taking them from the friars and selling them to whoever would buy them.

At that date the successes and failures had fairly well sorted themselves out. San Luis Rey was thriving, with 2,800 neophytes, 27,500 head of cattle, 26,100 sheep, and 1,300 goats. San José, San Diego, and San Gabriel were doing about half as well, with Santa Clara not far behind. Eight other missions were clearly in trouble, with fewer than 400 neophytes, while the rest were barely surviving.

The situation was much the same in Arizona. San Xavier del Bac was completed soon before 1800, and the large Franciscan church at Tumacácori that we see today (its predecessor, a Jesuit chapel, is present only in its foundations) was commenced in 1802. Like the Alamo, it was never completed. The seventeenth-century missions among the Hopi had been abandoned for a century. It is wondrous that the Franciscans persisted for so long after the chain of abortive little missions along the Gila River had failed and the Pima or Apache had burned out a succession of missionary entries into Arizona's bitter, arid land. In 1804 a head count found about a thousand "Hispanic" people around Tucson and San Xavier, about a hundred at Tubac, and eighty-two *gente de raison* (a term wonderfully expressive of Spanish attitudes toward the other *gente*, the natives) in the garrisons at Tubac and Tumacácori.

San Xavier was completed just as the ten-year struggle for Mexican independence began. Most of the creole aristocrats who led that movement, like their counterparts among the American Founding Fathers, were hostile to the power of the Church, and support for the missions flagged. Those loyal to Spain allocated their scarce resources to the royal armies, not to subsidizing friars. Texas was a lost cause: the friars were starving, the missions deserted. The composite society of New Mexico was, to all intents, independent already. Arizona was scarcely penetrated, and in California the missions were subsidizing the government, not the other way around. During one of the turns of the revolutionary wheel in Spain itself, a liberal parliament announced that the missions would be turned over to their parishioners in 1813. Though a returning monarch reversed the decree, it was enforced in some places on the frontier and was made a plank in the program of Mexico's "liberator," Agustín de Iturbide. Conservatives, such as General Santa Anna, attempted to reverse the situation by inviting the Jesuits back, but his initiative failed. By the end of the 1830s secularization, meaning selling off to ranchers, sutlers, and speculators, was complete except in one or two remote places where the parishioners would not hear of it and had the power to enforce their views. The mission was carried forward by saints and sinners, serving and being served by others who also included saints and sinners. Sometimes human aspiration and ambition alone took center stage. Sometimes the mission was purified into service alone with the crucified Christ as the example.

The imperial domes of San Xavier del Bac, near Tucson, Arizona.

PART I
THE RELIGIOUS MISSION

BETWEEN THE TANGIBLE AND THE INTANGIBLE

WE WILL RETURN TO ARCHITECTURE AND TO POLITICS. Before we do, however, a due respect for those who built the missions requires of us that we try to see them as they saw themselves, as instruments of faith.

Missions were built for several purposes, some of which were entirely secular. Their builders were of many sorts, and many who labored upon them did so under compulsion. But these are not secular buildings, nor were they intended to serve routine functions. They were created to disrupt routine and to provide occasions of grace.

At their best, the mission builders went to the political frontier — and many of them died there — to create opportunities for their fellow humans to cross a spiritual frontier.

All churches stand on a frontier. "Al tegabee" — "Nolo me tangere!" — "Do not touch me!" Christ said when he was no longer Jesus and had crossed the frontier. Visible and audible but no longer tangible, He admonished his disciples neither to cross the line unbidden nor to attempt to draw Him back to their side of the line, back into their world, where things are tested for truth by touching them.

In Christian belief, Christ was an intervention into their world, changing it though not changing its forms. Unlike many of the beliefs of the people among whom the missions were established, Christianity is a historical religion. It is important to Christians that Jesus was born, lived, and died. Equally important in their theology, however, is the belief that His historical crossing of that frontier from the tangible to the intangible was not the end of the story. He returned.

This is much to believe. And there is more. Neither his going across nor his returning were once for always, like the passage of a meteor through a planetary system. Crossings and recrossings recur. They are going on at this instant, sometimes in churches, sometimes at unmarked points.

Almost nothing can be said with certainty about grace, beyond the assertion that it is unpredictable. Nonetheless, Christians believe that there are ways to make grace more likely. Churches, especially mission churches, are arranged as containers for occasions of a heightened likelihood of grace called sacraments. Baptistries and sacristies and chapels serve as retorts (in the chemical sense), gathering those forces that may benignly breach the orderly sequences of physics, thereby disrupting cause and effect.

At Communion (in some denominations called the Eucharist), for example, the gifts of the earth — wheat and the juice of grapes — are first transformed into bread and wine, then, with the catalysis of faith, into flesh and blood. That is quite a lot of change, but it does not yet go beyond the frontier: everything is still tangible. Then — the true recurrent miracle — the tangible gives nutriment to the spirit.

Other sacraments are of equal wonder when they work. So are prayers, crossing in one direction, and grace, in the other. Christians believe that these transactions are going on all the time, and not only among Christians.

Some of the people who constructed the buildings depicted in these pages believed all this.

The sharp edge of a church tower against the sky: we can see it clearly enough as a metaphor, a thing set against the airy realm of nonthings. The intention of an entire church building, a bulky object, is not so easy to read. We have been trained since the Renaissance to see it in perspective, to parse its physics, weigh its ceilings, press against its walls, test its floors, analyze the influences of its forms, talk before we feel, discourse before we understand. Although the mission churches in these pages were constructed at a time when plenty of attention was given to things — there was plenty of avarice and lust and gluttony in the world — nonthings were more important then than they are now. All the battalions of tangibilities had not yet been mobilized to insist that we ignore everything else. Perspective in painting, realism in literature, science as a religion — these were not yet fully ascendant.

When we enter these churches it is helpful to remember that when they were built the most important function of religious architecture was to serve religion, that is, to resist the tyranny of the thing, of the present moment and of momentary desire. These buildings are incomprehensible if we come to them as we would to a laboratory or a university barracks for the soldiers of science, with their auxiliaries of social science stabled just outside.

It is especially important that we not read the images in these buildings as illustrations in a textbook, as if they must all be pictures of something. The primary function of the religious art found here is not representation but metaphor. The sculptures in polychrome and plaster, in niches, on twisted pillars, populating doorways and some of the more extravagant windows are metaphors as well. The massed metaphors upon the retablos behind the altars, especially, are not to be taken literally.

Opposite: Controlling time: bells, domes, and supremacy. The bell tower at San Ignacio de Caburica, Sonora, Mexico.

No one is saying to us that Jesus looked like *that*, or that Almighty God looks like that. These painted figures are economical. They do only what they are intended to do, with the means at their disposal. They offer some suggestions about mysteries so vast as to exceed our understanding, and our understanding of that understanding — and they do so diffidently.

The closest analogues to these figures are not botanical drawings but the icons of the Eastern Orthodox Church and the larger icons deployed upon the mosaic ceilings of the surviving Byzantine churches in Sicily and Venice. None of these are meant to depict any *thing*; they are meant to induce us to imagine what certain nonthings might be like. Rather than *objects* at which our gaze terminates, they are apertures. They are not painted shutters but open windows.

Painted ceilings, in Mexico or New Mexico, like the Mediterranean mosaics that preceded them, draw the eye upward and invite attention past and through the ceiling. They encourage the fervent to believe away that surface, to burn it into a powder that will float into space and leave the sun and moon and the other wonders of the heavens visible.

The history of the Mexican-American retablo probably began with the Third Provincial Councils in 1585, which confirmed the adherence of the churches of the Western Hemisphere to the Counter Reformation. Soon thereafter, churches began to present screens that combined painting, sculpture, and architecture to intensify the verbal instruction of the congregation. It is often said that these composite teaching screens emphasized narrative. Certainly they did. But they also humanized theology, providing in images a directness, a sense of personal caring, to the rather general theories of the Erasmian intellectuals among the Jesuits drawn to Mexico after the first twelve apostolic friars.

These paintings must do the work of the stained glass of northern churches. Light is used sparingly in hot countries, for it is too much like heat. Lovers of the Gothic stained glass of northern Europe will not find much of it in these missions. There is plenty of Gothicism in Mexico, and even a little in California, but it is not the light-filled Gothicism of Rheims, York, or Sainte-Chapelle. The religious iconography of the missions does not come to us shrouded in the vagueness of Gothic light, tinctured and dissolved and softened by sunlight filtering through colored glass.

Consequently, though the art of the Mediterranean, of Mexico, and of the missions sometimes seems garish to northern eyes, it is merely straightforward.

Indeed, it is interesting that in the missions north of the present Mexican-American border there is little use of the Baroque tricks with light that came *after* the Renaissance, Counter Reformation devices intended to replenish the depleted supply of mystery in Catholic churches. The Jesuit church of San Martin at Tepotztlán, near Mexico City, is one of the greatest testaments to the Baroque and the Counter Reformation in the world, and to theatrical lighting. But this approach did not carry over to the frontier churches, except, perhaps, for the practice of raising the nave a little above the sanctuary so as to permit natural light from above to fall upon the altar. (One can see this device at the mission church at Trampas, New Mexico, which was constructed in 1991 entirely in accord with the preferences of the congregation.)

Even in Mexico, the churches at the farthest reach of Catholic Europe were too straightforward to offer the carefully contrived surprises of Central European Baroque, such as light from hidden sources emerging from behind the whipped-cream ornament. Straightforwardness does not, however, mean that these interiors are prosaic. At San Xavier del Bac in Arizona, light from the windows in the drum streams across the dark interior space and strikes the saints in their niches as the sun moves overhead during the Mass.

The missions within the present boundaries of the United States were constructed after the Baroque was in full flower in Europe. The muscular striving of Baroque ornament is there in mission sculpture, especially in the Texas missions and at San Xavier del Bac, but the Baroque had no effect whatever upon the shaping of buildings and little upon the uses of light.

The remaining Jesuit ruins remind us that in the Pimería Alta (the region encompassing present-day northern Sonora and southern Arizona) the Franciscans and Jesuits favored different materials: the Jesuits used for their masonry churches only sun-dried adobes and mud mortar; the Franciscans, arriving later, used kiln-dried brick and lime mortar.

The adobe remains of Los Santos Angeles de Guevavi, south of Tucson, a Kino church abandoned in 1771.

Even at their most opulent, the frontier missions are not fancy. They arise from different circumstances than those expressed in the flamboyant Baroque of Mexico's mining boom towns. As the proprietors of the mines returned to architecture some of the wealth extracted from the sweat of Indians and the accumulated minerals of the earth, they redeployed gold and silver in encrusting ornament behind the main altar and in side chapels. The floor plans of churches such as those at Zacatecas, Taxco, and Guanajuato, cruciform and domed, are attributable less to the soldier-priests of the Society of Jesus than to a new Mexican bourgeoisie aspiring to become aristocrats.

Nothing of this sort was seen in the Jesuit provinces of the rough Sierra Madre, in the canyons of Sinaloa and Sonora, or in Baja. Even when the Franciscans of Arizona built their great Baroque church at San Xavier, and their confreres in Texas attempted to match it with the group of churches around San Antonio, the American missions were obviously frontier buildings.

Although the resources assembled to build these churches were huge by the standards of the Indians of those areas, they were meager indeed compared to those of the silver cities and urban centers in the Valley of Mexico. In the north, missionaries could not be wasteful if waste meant confusion. Their message had to be clear. Though that message was mysterious, it was not meant to be baffling. It might be complex — a multitude of metaphors is assembled in each retablo — but it had to be intelligible.

The retablo was a signpost at the frontier of the intangible, like the iconostasis of an Eastern Orthodox cathedral. Simple does not mean primitive, in Arizona or in Kiev or in Monreale. The Byzantine liturgy and the Eastern Orthodox tradition that ensues from it occur in interiors quite like those of the missions. Sunlight is banished, and candles flicker against gilded screens bearing signs leading to the most sophisticated truths of human experience; the flickering reminds us how little we can see into the abyss of the mystery of life.

Some people are baffled by the flatness of many of these painted metaphors. Amid the haze of incense, as deep-throated incantations sound repeated phrases of an ancient liturgy, this flatness conveys its intended meaning to those who gaze upon it with symbolic contemplation, though some people trained in the Renaissance tradition are so offended by the absence of modeling that they offer it as proof that those who made the paintings were "primitive."

Above:
The resurrection remains beyond the cross, life beyond death. The retablo of Nuestra Señora de la Asunción at Zia Pueblo, New Mexico.

Many icons in missions are painted flat on a gold background, like those in the churches of the Eastern Rite. That is how they have been created for well over fifteen hundred years, as the result of the deliberate decision of the artists of Byzantium no longer to paint classically. They relinquished the tricks of modeling — the darkening of the edges of a figure to suggest a backward curve — and perspective — the placement of a figure in the midst of the optical illusion created by lines converging to suggest distance. Greek and Roman artists had educated their clients to accept these devices and to be beguiled away from the evidence of their eyes that the canvases and frescoed walls before them were flat. Classical art purveyed illusion.

Byzantine artists ceased playing tricks with perspective; their clients did not require the amusement of trompe l'oeil. They were aware that the world before them had sufficient illusions, chiefly the permanence of objects and the viewer's eternal life amid such objects. In the presence of the ephemera of life, the Byzantines agreed not to be amused by visual tricks. They were serious people: life is fleeting, and all material things decay, we ourselves among them. So our icons — our *santos* and retablos — are invitations not to spatial amusements but to eternal things, beyond space because beyond time.

This deliberate flatness was not a primitive notion. When flatness was rejected by the secularism of the Renaissance, art recoiled from the contemplation of mystery. Rejoicing once again in games of perspective and modeling, art celebrated those transiencies of the "real world" — the world of objects rather than subjects — that the Byzantines rejected as trivial. This change must have come as a relief; during the Middle Ages, Europe had lived constantly on the frontier, aware of both worlds at once, always teetering on the edge of an abyss. Only saints can live for very long like that without vertigo. The rest of us grasp for objects, for the tangible. The Renaissance encouraged people to think they could live nearly all the time in just one world, that of the tangible.

What has this to do with missions? Or with the religious mission that is the subject of this chapter? Only this: we should be wary of writers who use the word "primitive" too readily when they are dealing with metaphors. Icons and retablos may require more of the painter and of the observer than the most virtuosic of painted illusions. The purpose of a beginning is not the same as the purpose of an end.

Above:
Murals at San Diego del Pitiquito, Sonora. Grandeur and irony are intermingled in the Hispanic traditon. There may be majesty in heaven, but life on earth is brief, and ultimately all humankind comes to a common end.

BETWEEN TWO
RELIGIOUS SYSTEMS

MANKIND HAS CREATED BUILDINGS to mediate between the tangible and the intangible in many climates and upon many topographies. Sometimes these buildings are called churches, mosques, or temples, sometimes missions, but in all of them humans, bound to space and time, have sought means of escape from both space and time.

One method of escape from the body is through mortification of the flesh. The escape is from the body itself, from the toucher as well as the touched. This mode was important in Europe before the invasion of America, especially among the Franciscans. Among the Indian nations in America a practice, similar in its bloody physical effects but very different in purpose, seems to have been widespread in the Southwest and along the Missouri River (see page 104). We note these practices here because depictions of flagellation and of bloody vestments are shocking to many mission visitors. This may be a therapeutic shock; it may shatter some preconceptions.

Religion was not a European, or even a Near Eastern, invention. The American missions were introduced into a place that already demonstrated a very active religious life. When European ideas of how religion should be practiced are used to interpret Native American practices, all sorts of errors creep in. Some of these errors can be avoided if one admits that religious ideas, if not missionary activity, have gone in both directions. At first, as the mission churches demonstrate, the traffic in ideas ran from Europe toward America; in our day some religious conceptions are seeping, without evangelism, in the other direction.

America was not an empty continent — not empty of people or of religious concepts. In 1492 there were probably as many people living in the Western Hemisphere as there were in western Europe. Aztec Mexico City was the most prosperous, glamorous, and beautiful city in Europe or America. Paris and Naples may have been more populous, but they were squalid and ugly by comparison.

These Americans already had a religious life. Judging from the liturgical objects they have left to us, that religious life had its

own sacraments. Judging from what their descendants tell us, their liturgies were as elaborate and invocatory as those of the Christians.

The missions, therefore, were *intercessions* between two cultures, not merely *extensions* of one. This is an important distinction; it is a solvent for such words as "outposts" and for the use on maps of great white spaces surrounding a great blob of Spanish orange in central Mexico, with orange-and-white stripes edging warily out toward Santa Fe, San Francisco, and the Alamo. (Mapmakers seem to think of Spanish occupation as faintly burned around the edges — perhaps the auto-da-fé lurks unconscious in the choice.)

White space suggests that nothing was there. But something *was* there. The Indians brought their religion into the mission compounds as they labored under the direction of the friars, sometimes in the presence of armored men on horseback, sometimes happy to be paid for the work of making the buildings. They brought their religion into the sanctuaries built for the friars as they brought it into the sanctuaries they continued to build for themselves.

A full account of the diversity of Indian religions, as practiced while the missions were being built and as practiced today, would have to be very long and very detailed, using many words not found in English. Here I will simply emphasize this unifying theme: like some forms of early Christianity, these religions treated objects and animals as partaking in the sacred. That is to say, they did *not* treat human nature as being separate from and superior to the rest of nature.

It is not easy for humans to treat one another as participating in sacredness. It is harder still to treat creatures beyond our species with that sort of respect. An open-armed address to the rest of creation has not been a prominent theme in modern Christianity, even among those who read literally the unbroken sequence of creation in the Book of Genesis.

Above: La Isabela, Columbus's colony on Hispaniola, had the first Christian church built in the New World since those of the Vikings on Greenland. Not a mission church in the ecclesiastical sense, since it was only for the garrison, it was an instrument of the overall mission of colonization.

The Indians remind us that ours is an impoverished Christianity; our gratitude to God used to be more encompassing. Fortunately, history offers us renewable opportunities to learn from others. One reason for composing this book is the hope that we all may benefit from a reinvigoration of the ample view of sacredness held by those people among whom the missions were placed.

To suggest what might be found in an anthology of a capacious Christianity, I offer three quotations. The first is from a contemporary American Indian theologian, the second from an old-fashioned Irish Catholic, and the third from the first Franciscan.

Here is Audrey Shenandoah, an Onondaga, speaking to the Global Forum on Environment and Development for Survival, in Moscow, January 1990:

> Now our words we direct to our Mother Earth, who supports all life. . . . We include all the plant life, the woodlands, all the waters of Earth, the fishes, the animal life, the bird life, and the Four Winds. As one mind our acknowledgment, respect, and thanksgiving move upward to the Sky World: the Grandmother Moon, who has a direct relationship to the females of the species of all living things, the sun and the stars; and our Spiritual Beings of the Sky World.

Here is a stanza from an ancient prayer from Ireland, traditionally called "The Shield of Saint Patrick."

> For my shield this day I call:
> Heaven's might,
> Sun's brightness,
> Moon's whiteness,
> Fire's glory,
> Lightning's swiftness,
> Wind's wildness,
> Ocean's depth,
> Earth's solidity,
> Rock's immobility.

And here are a few stanzas from the most famous of the prayers of Saint Francis, composed early in the thirteenth century.

> Be thou praised, my Lord, with all Thy creatures,
> Above all Brother Sun,
> who gives the day and brightens us therewith . . .
> Be thou praised, my Lord, of Sister Moon and the stars;
> in the heaven hast thou formed them, clear and precious and comely.
>
> Be thou praised, my Lord, of Brother Wind,
> and of the air, and the clouds, and of fair and of all weather, by which Thou givest to thy creatures sustenance.
>
> Be thou praised, my Lord, of Sister Water,
> which is much useful and humble and precious and pure.
>
> Be thou praised, my Lord, of Brother Fire,
> by which Thou hast lightened the night,
> and he is beautiful and joyful and robust and strong.
>
> Be thou praised, my Lord, of our Sister Earth,
> which sustains and hath us in rule,
> and produces divers fruits with colored flowers and herbs.

PART II
THE PARTICIPANTS

WHO WERE THE INDIANS?

THE GREAT SCHOLARLY DEBATE about the number of people living in the Western Hemisphere in 1492 has not been settled, but many of us are now satisfied that there were about fifty million. A succession of demographic studies has persuaded us that Columbus found nearly two million on the populous island of Hispaniola, of which only about sixteen thousand were left a century later. In other parts of the New World the rate of loss of life was not so high, but it is safe to say that the Great Dying of the sixteenth century was the largest catastrophe in human history. It was followed by a succession of localized dyings as European and African diseases spread through populations sufficiently isolated to have been spared the first. The last of these did not complete its devastations in remote villages of the far north until our own time.

The people of the Americas were as various as the Europeans who came among them, as various as the people of Africa. They included some very small people, such as the four-and-a-half-foot-high Motilón, as well as the Kiowa and Sioux, who were thought to be giants by the five-and-a-half-foot-tall Frenchmen who first saw them. They included the people of Florida and Texas, depicted by the first European painters as towering over the Spaniards. Jean Beranger, who explored the Texas coast for France, reported that around Aransas Bay he saw "tall, plump and shapely" people who ranged from five foot five to six foot two. European Americans who saw the same Karankawa in the 1830s reported that some were over six feet and that the alligator fat with which they smeared themselves made them "hideous" and unbearably smelly. (Europeans did not, in general, find Indians insufficiently fastidious; on the contrary, the natives were astonishingly willing to assume the risks of bathing more than once a week.) A recent summary of Indian groups in California asserts that the area contained "both the tallest and shortest native groups in North America." Given what we know of the Motilón and Karankawa, and occasional unconfirmed sightings of Sioux at six foot three, that is quite a statement.

Yet it is probably true, and with it the equally remarkable assertion that California contained sixty tribes speaking ninety languages. Elsewhere both the Arawak and the Natchez had different languages for people of different status, so the Californians' linguistic diversity is thoroughly credible. A map of language distribution in North America before the arrival of the Europeans must be carefully dated. In the tenth century, for example, there were no Apache or Navajo in the Southwest; the mysterious Zuñi tongue was probably already being spoken by other groups, now departed, though no other nation now shares the Zuñi way of speaking. In the singularity of their languages, the Zuñi are the Basques of the desert, as the Calusa in southern Florida and the Karankawa in coastal Texas were the Basques of their regions.

Perhaps these groups have always spoken isolated languages, but perhaps, like the Yuchi of Tennessee, the Keres-speaking people of Acoma and Laguna, New Mexico, and the Yuki-Wappo of the Great Valley of California, they are speaking languages that predate the great Ice Age, about 18,000 B.C. That event separated the residents of North America from one another for six millennia. In recent years linguists, folk historians, and archaeologists have correlated the dispersion

of languages and the dispersion of animals and plants from the refuges in which they waited out the glaciers. The results of these studies are very exciting.

As the ice thawed, people and animals were free once again to move. Aleuts and Eskimos, living in an extension of Siberia covering much of Alaska and blocked by ice from the rest of America, spread out eastward as far as Greenland, where they ultimately encountered Europeans. A multitude of Nadene-speaking peoples, having diversified their languages during the long glacial hiatus, spread into those portions of Alaska and the northwest provinces of Canada uncontested by the Aleut-Eskimo coalition. Much later, in historic times, some of them, the Navajo and Apache, drove down the eastern side of the Rocky Mountains, crossed into New Mexico, and commenced their long process of competition and accommodation with the inhabitants of the pueblos.

California in ancient times was a polyglot province, as it was when the friars came into it and as it is today. It has always been the most cosmopolitan region of the United States and the most confusing. It was fecund in languages, in diversity of cultures, and in puzzles for sociologists.

Impacted south of the glacial sheet, in the Mississippi Valley, there seem to have been two bands of Indian life. One area, inhabited by the ancestors of the Algonkian speakers, was a region of mixed deciduous and coniferous forests; as the ice melted, the climate warmed and the region acquired more and more of the deciduous woods, some remnants of which still remain in the defiles of the Ozarks and the Cumberland Plateau. South of this area was probably the homeland of the Caddoan-Iroquoian-Siouan-speaking people. Some of the Biloxi, Cherokee, and Caddo still inhabit enclaves of their ancient habitat in the Gulf plains. The Dakota and Wyandot migrated, sometimes willingly, as far as Canada, and the Crow went as far as the headwaters of the Missouri-Mississippi system, driving the Algonkian speakers ahead of them. This suggested reconstruction of events far beyond the horizon of the known satisfies many of the puzzles involved in laying out a sequence of events in the distant past. Although the language groupings reported by Europeans in 1492 bear no relationship to the neat rectangles into which the Congress of the United States subsequently divided our part of the continent, there were people who could understand each other distributed across most of the major geographical provinces after the departure of the glaciers.

Because of these dislocations from common bases, it was possible that a person who grew up in the St. Lawrence Valley might be understood if he or she traveled to the Great Basin, the southeastern sand plains, the midwestern prairies, or the Florida peninsula. But not likely. There were forty languages within the Athapaskan linguistic grouping alone.

The Indians did not talk alike, act alike, nor look alike. There were blue-eyed and brown-haired Mandan. There were people with yellowish, reddish, and brownish skin, with thin lips and thick lips, with round heads and long heads, with Siouan or "Roman" noses and flat, snub noses — "Carthaginian" perhaps?

Some people lived very well in large villages and produced complex architecture, hardly bothering to farm. Among these were the salmon-fishing people of the Northwest Coast, the whale-hunting Chumash of the horn of California, near Santa Barbara, and the Calusa of Florida, for whom nature provided so well that it was not cost-effective to grow crops. Some equivalently complex societies produced equivalently grand architecture based upon the culture of corn, squash, and beans.

Of the communities large enough to be characterized as "urban," within what is now the United States, the most dramatic were those clustered around Cahokia and St. Louis in the eleventh through the fourteenth century, and those in the San Juan and Delores valleys of Colorado in the ninth century. In both cases, the population of these urban centers exceeded those of London or Rome at the time. In Mexico and Central America, the urban achievements of the Aztec and Maya were so astonishing that it would be fair to say that compared to them all others, including the Spaniards, were barbarians.

Immediately upon their arrival in the Americas, Europeans put the people they found here to work. After one generation, only a small percentage of the people who had lived in the West Indies remained. Perhaps four out of five had died from disease or overwork in mines and farms. The Europeans then turned to Africa for a work force, importing with its black slaves new microbial enemies that killed nearly all of the remaining natives of the Caribbean.

As the islands became depopulated, soldiers and priests landed on the mainland. There, for the first time, the invaders encountered a heavily settled, urban, civilized, stratified society ruled by a military elite. The experience of the Spaniards with the Moors had equipped them for this; they knew how to play upon local feuds and to acquire enough allies to substitute their own elite for the elite they decapitated and to resume its role in extracting labor from the peasantry.

As the Spaniards moved northward, however, they found the native population much more scattered and less accustomed to following orders even from its own chiefs. For several centuries the Spaniards remained at war with these people. While there were interludes of accommodation by urban groups such as those of the Rio Grande pueblos, the Spaniards' secular exploitation, religious intolerance, and incuriousness about sociology led to revolts even on the part of these people. The Pueblo Revolt of 1680 drove out the Spanish soldiers and missionaries. Out they stayed for twelve years, until they understood that they would have to live in mutual accommodation with the Pueblos. At the same time the Pueblos were persuaded that a reformed Spanish rule was preferable to what the newly arrived Apache would do to them if they were left undefended.

The Chichimaca and the Teochichemec of northern Mexico never were convinced that the net effect of missions and their accompanying garrisons would be benign, and they fought the Spaniards for four centuries. The Apache and the Comanche of Texas adopted the same policy, as did the Sioux and Cheyenne, after bitter lessons, toward the westering Americans.

A detail from a pre-Columbian Mayan mural.

La Purísima Concepción de Quarai.

WHO WERE THE SPANIARDS?

LET US LOOK MORE CLOSELY at the people we have been calling the Spaniards. A glance at any portrait of Queen Isabella of Castile (1451–1504) reminds us of her lineage. Like her cousin (several times removed) Elizabeth of England (1533–1603), she had auburn hair and blue-green eyes. She was, indeed, almost as English a lady as the predominantly Welsh "Queen Bess."

The dynasties of England and Spain had long made war and love against and with each other. Edward, "the Black Prince" (1330–1376), clawed his way through the Pyrenees from his satrapy in Aquitaine, conducting his own peninsular campaign five centuries before the Duke of Wellington. At the end, Edward was among those who set Pedro (Peter) the Cruel back upon the throne of Castile.

(This was less of a gift to fourteenth-century Castilians than to twentieth-century readers, for it permitted a later Englishman, Walter Alison Phillips, to deliver the choicest line of invective in all of the volumes of the *Encyclopaedia Britannica* of 1911. Writing of Pedro IV of Aragon, Phillips wrote: "He was a typical king of the . . . century, immeasurably false, and unspeakably ferocious, but he was not a mere bloodthirsty sultan like his enemy, Peter [Pedro] the Cruel of Castile.")

Pedro the Cruel had to fend off a claim upon the throne of Castile by John of Gaunt, based upon his marriage to Pedro's eldest daughter. Gaunt settled the matter by providing a daughter to be queen; this made him an ancestor of Isabella of Castile, who was both cousin and wife to Ferdinand of Aragon. (Gaunt was, in fact, Isabella's ancestor twice, the second time through a daughter who became a Portuguese princess.) In their union, these cousins united the Spanish kingdoms.

It is often forgotten that Spain and England were thereafter allies against a common enemy, France, until they were separated by their differing responses to the Reformation. In 1495, as Columbus was building the first Catholic church in the New World at La Isabela, England joined with the Spanish kingdoms, the papacy, and the Holy Roman Empire in what these still Catholic powers delighted in calling their Holy League against France.

As late as 1554, only the fallibility of human procreation denied to the marriage of Philip of Spain and Mary Tudor, queen of England, a recreated Anglo-Spanish alliance in Europe and America. Mary was barren; after she died in 1558, Elizabeth, a firm Protestant and an implacable sponsor of colonies and pirates, became queen. As we shall observe, those who suffered most grievously from that event were the Indians of New Mexico and Florida.

The accidents of history and of human sexuality confuse the neat categories of race and nationality, especially in Spain and Spanish America. There were blue-eyed caliphs in Córdoba, the offspring of unions between members of Moorish royal families and blond women from Galicia (*gallegos*); the Arabs did not at first bring their women to Spain, nor did the Spaniards bring theirs to Mexico and New Spain. The great Arab chieftain and ravager of Santiago de Compostela, al-Mansur, had two Christian wives; the daughter of the caliph of Seville married Alfonso VI of Castile and Leon. The Christian and Muslim aristocracies intermarried frequently, following the precedents of kings and caliphs, and these mingled genes were mingled once again with those of the Jewish advisers to both royal lines. The mother of Ferdinand of Aragon, Juana Enriquez, was a product of this triple heritage.

The word "Moorish" really should be in quotation marks because it means "derived from Morocco" or perhaps Mauretania, and in many ways Morocco was more an obstacle to the transmission of Muslim culture than a seedbed. It was occupied by the Berbers, many of whom resisted Arab influences, while others converted to Islam and joined in the conquest of the primary Arab objective, fertile Spain. Architecture flourished in Spain, as it did in the Arab lands; back from Spain to Morocco came the fused style we often call "Moorish." The style conquered Morocco culturally after it was already established in Spain.

Opposite: The Alcazar Castle, Queen Isabella's residence.

People may have lived in Spain 25,000 years ago, and certainly did 15,000 years ago, creating at Altamira the finished, accurate, polychrome depictions of the animals with which they shared the Spanish landscape. These people left evidence of hunting with bows. They were, therefore, more technologically advanced than their North American counterparts, who did not paint so well and did not use bows until about 800 A.D. Otherwise there does not seem to have been much difference in the lifeways on the two sides of the Atlantic for most of human history. Finally, about 5,000 years ago, North Africans (Egyptians) learned to play flutes, harps, lyres, and double clarinets; to smelt bronze, gold, and silver; and, along with the Sumerians, to write. Sometime within the next 2,000 years Levantine sailors brought those skills to Spain.

Spain was a melting pot, with many Levantine and African admixtures. Africans called Capsians, after the principal location of their art, Capsa, now Gafsa, in Tunisia created the second period of Spanish painting, depicting humans fighting, dancing, and gesturing lubriciously. Next came more middle easterners, who, with the Altamirans and Capsians were members of the group we call Mediterranean. These castle builders were of medium height, curly-haired, slender, and dark-skinned. While Americans along the Washita River of Louisiana had been building monumental earthen buildings since 3000 B.C., and as they laid up great earthen and shell circles such as that at Poverty Point, Louisiana (about 1000 B.C.), and Fort Center, Florida (about the time of Homer, 850 B.C.), and the British were creating stone circles such as that at Stonehenge, the Mediterraneans were presiding over the Spanish Bronze Age.

In the ninth century B.C. the Celtic ancestors of the beguiling *gallegos* arrived, sturdy, tall, square-headed, blond, and blue-eyed. Their descendants are sometimes encountered, somewhat unexpectedly, in the mountains of Galicia, in Argentina, and in Mexico. In Spain they are said to account for an equally unexpected hard-headedness in business in equally remote places. This may be unfair to the Phoenicians and Carthaginians, who preceded the Romans to Spain. They, too, were canny traders, and they brought darker skins and slender physiques.

"Roman Spain" is something of a misnomer, encouraged by architectural history, which provides trays of slides of theaters, prodigious aqueducts, viaducts, bridges, and multitudes of columns, which were reused by the Visigoths, Moors, and Christians. We are induced to believe that these structures must have been built by a multitude of Romans, but that was not the case. Spain had Roman garrisons, Roman retirement communities, Roman merchants, Roman poets and philosophers, but it never had a great many of them, and they stayed in their cities and villas, seldom venturing to mix with the mass of the people.

The same can be said of the Visigoths, who succeeded the Romans as military overlords. There were probably no more Visigoths in Spain than there were Jews at the time. When the Moors came in the eighth century, they brought even more Jews with them. The Jews took a central role in the intellectual and commercial life of the country, while the big, hairy, leek-eating, bluff, hearty Visigothic fullbacks eschewed such matters and, for all purposes beyond invidious genealogy among Spanish aristocrats, died out.

We must, however, record here an architectural legacy left to the Americas by the Visigoths: the horseshoe arch and combinations of horseshoe arches, such as those appearing in colonnades in Yucatán. Historians have not picked up persuasive prototypes for the Visigothic horseshoe arch in the earlier work of either the Romans or the Iberians.

As to the Jewish strain in Spanish life, the economic historian Jaime Vicens Vives has pointed out that "the Spanish Jew of the thirteenth century was identical to a Spanish Christian of the same time, except in two important things — he had a different religion and a very different economic mentality." So when we speak of the Jewish strain in the Spanish royal family, it is not to suggest any distinctive physical quality.

Opposite: The mission at Pecos, New Mexico. Arches like these could be seen in Babylon by the time of the Babylonian captivity of the Jews, but they did not appear in America until after 1492.

Above: Horseshoe arches in La Mezquita,
the Great Mosque of Abdar Rahman.

The term "Moor" is also subject to fracture at the touch. It does not very well describe the Arab monarchs who first came to Spain; it may be more useful in denoting their successors, the Berbers, a composite people composed of elements of dark-skinned sub-Saharan stock, of Syrians, and of Egyptians. Among the Moors who came into Spain, at least five times as many were Berbers as Arabs. Most of these immigrants, including nearly all the 40,000 Arabs among them, came without women, so the admixtures soon became bewildering.

Then came the Vikings, who took Cádiz twice in the tenth century, at the same time that they were expanding their base on Greenland toward Vinland. Viking genes were available along the coast of Spain for a century or more thereafter. Finally, and perhaps most important, was the French invasion. In the Middle Ages the Pyrenees became porous. Overpopulated Gaul decanted its surplus into the cities of northern Spain, and the "Spanish" heartland, the steppes of Estremadura and Castile, were for the first time settled — by French, Catalans, and Basques. What language did shepherds first attempt as they came upon each other in windswept passes in those days? And what language was heard on the docks when, only a few decades later, that heartland sent forth its sons — once again, just its sons — to conquer America?

From its extraordinary admixture of peoples Spain derived much of its strength. Perhaps more than any other state in western Europe, it was ready for America. The little colonies of French, Basques, and Catalans in Castile and of Castilians, Catalans, and Aragonese scattered throughout the Muslim landscape of Andalusia prefigured the little communities of their grandchildren scattered throughout Mexico, and of the descendants of those grandchildren in Arizona, Texas, and New Mexico.

A resurgence of interest in Jewish learning has recently appeared in New Mexico, not limited to those of the Jewish intellectual tradition who came as Spaniards. That tradition has a proud lineage. Córdoba was, under the Muslims, the great center of Jewish intellectual life, centering around its Talmudic school. The minister of finance to the Moorish King Abdar Rahman III was Hisdai ibn-Shaprut. Samuel ha-Nagid was vizier to the king of Granada, and another Jew was vizier to the king of Saragossa. (Browning's celebrated Rabbi ben Ezra came later.)

Let us call them all Spaniards, those conquistadors in shining casques and breastplates, mounted upon superb gray stallions, although they were not all dark-bearded and dark-eyed. Cortés himself was an impoverished *hidalgo* from Estremadura. But men of several nations stood beside him as he dedicated upon the Mexican coast a new city named for the true cross (Veracruz). Was he a Jew, a Muslim, or a Christian who followed the order of Cortés to set afire the floating fortresses that had brought them there, to forbid retreat? Who conquered Mexico for Catholic Europe? Flemings and Portuguese, French, Germans, Italians — and Spaniards.

THE MODERNITY OF MEDIEVAL SPAIN

Spain was considerably more diverse and more "modern" than any state could be if populated only by swashbuckling knights or shepherds. The core of the realm of Ferdinand of Aragon was Catalonia, centered upon the city of Barcelona. The textile capital of the western Mediterranean, Barcelona was fiercely engaged in commercial relations as far as the Levant. The Aragonese were not isolated country gentlemen or knights-at-arms. They operated a commercial system that even exceeded the bounds of their political empire, which stretched to include the duchy of Athens, the metropolis of Naples, and the islands of Sardinia and Sicily. Long before the Hapsburgs incorporated Flanders and Spain into the same empire, Spanish traders were swarming through trade fairs, haggling and bickering from Bruges to Alexandria.

Spain's readiness for the modern age came in part from the contentious, irrepressible individuality of the peoples of the fiefs ruled by the royal cousins, Ferdinand and Isabella. A docile Spain, homogenized or drilled into the sort of imperial monarchy attempted elsewhere in Europe, could not have made available people so fitted for independent action as Cortés, Pizarro, Menéndez de Avilés of Florida, or Oñate of New Mexico.

Even if we set aside the diversity of Spanish life, its intense precapitalist economy, and its cosmopolitanism, even if we focus only upon the mailed horseman, the dark-bearded conquistador of legend, it is important to distinguish him from those courtiers who thronged about the absolutist courts of Europe in other places and in later times. If he had been that, he never would have conquered America from Tierra del Fuego to Sonoma and Bodega Bay.

The great Peruvian man of letters Mario Vargas Llosa posed the question, how were a few hundred "semiliterate, implacable and greedy swordsmen" led by Pizarro able to gain dominance over twenty million Indians led by the Inca aristocracy? Among its other accomplishments, that aristocracy had created the world's most immense masonry architecture and a network of highways over thousands of miles and had eradicated hunger throughout the vast Andean region.

Vargas Llosa's answer was that the Inca empire, unlike the Spanish, was organized as a "vertical and totalitarian structure" whose citizens were "incapable of taking individual initiative" and whose religion "took away the individual's free will and crowned the authority's decision with an aura of divine mandate." One hundred eighty Spanish soldiers, each a unit to himself, attacked a "beehive — laborious, efficient, stoic." When the ruler was killed, the ruled knew no other life but the acceptance of a new ruler.

Whatever else he was, the Spanish *hidalgo* was not "laborious"; it was dishonorable for him to labor with his hands. Wealth was supposed to come from booty. It might go into herds of merino sheep, but in theory, the labor of the *hidalgo* was limited to cut and thrust. He was supposed to be "efficient" only in the use of weapons. The reality was quite different; though he may have been embarrassed by the necessity, many a *hidalgo* labored in shop or field. Still, as for "stoicism," he was as ready for the Service of Lamentation as for the auto-da-fé.

But he bent his knee to no man. It is inconceivable that Inca or Aztec nobles might presume as did the Aragonese who took the oath of allegiance to Ferdinand: "We who are as good as you swear to you, who are no better than we, to accept you as our king and sovereign lord, provided you observe all our liberties and laws; but if not, not."

In Castile, royal rule was felt primarily in the cities; the Moors had taught the Castilians the pleasures of urban life. There is a profound difference between the Spanish habit of colonizing village by village, with garrisons and clergy attached, and the farming tradition of the English colonists except, of course, the Londoners, who were few. As a result, no landscape in Latin America is anything like that of eighteenth-century Virginia.

The arches and columns of the twelfth-century synagogue in
Toledo.

WHY DID SPAIN LAG IN THE RACE INTO THE MODERN WORLD?

Not in every respect is it a good thing that we are no longer living in the Middle Ages. Courtly love has much to recommend it; artisanship is better than machine-multiplied shoddiness; and cathedrals are more beautiful than missile launchers. There was enough reality in the skein of mutual obligation of feudalism at its brief best to give rise to deep nostalgia in the hearts of pre-Raphaelites of all generations. Don Quixote is lovable; so are Hotspur and Henry VI. "Without fear and without reproach" would never do as an emblem for Drexel Burnham Lambert.

But here we are. Why did Spain take so long to join us? Why did it drop out of the race toward capitalism? Why did it become, by the nineteenth century, an isolated backwater of which the historian Vicens Vives noted that its "contribution to the general development of technology . . . has been minimal." Why, as a result, did the missions in Mexico and the American Southwest become capsules of a Spanish view of life as antipathetic as Spain itself to technological change, and perhaps to economic change as well?

By the time the missions began to be secularized in the 1790s, they were exhausted. Only their shells remained to be toppled by the Americans after 1850. The revival of the missions is, in all but a handful of cases, a twentieth-century phenomenon. Those within the present boundaries of the United States were constructed at a time when the rest of Europe, and Europe's American colonies (especially those of New England), were hastening toward industrialism and free markets. But the colonies of Spain, especially the little worlds of the mission compounds, turned their backs on all that.

Professor Lopez Ibor attributes Spain's recalcitrance to capitalism to the following factors: exhaustion from religious wars and imperial adventures; the Castilian's intensely personal view of economic relations and his "difficulty" in seizing such abstractions as the law of contract; "the bigotry of the concept of the hidalgo . . . the Spaniard's vocation for glory, both in battle and in literature; the sense of what is noble and hidalgesque; contempt for servile occupations and everything representing sustained labor." What Lopez Ibor calls "disinterestedness" is translated by Vicens Vives as "an absolute lack of curiosity. It stems from the conviction

that . . . we are the best, and furthermore the cleverest, of men, [and that] . . . our affairs are going very well."

These might be the qualities of a smug feudality of stay-at-homes being enriched by remittances sent by more energetic relatives in the colonies. It speaks for one group of Spanish aristocrats, whose scarcely altered views had disastrous consequences for Spain in the sixteenth century. It speaks, as well, for those churchmen who tried to "waterproof" the frontiers of the kingdom and its colonies against all forms of heresy, technological as well as religious and economic. Before we examine the means by which those relatives got into a position to *send* those remittances, we must ask why those churchmen were so powerful.

The Church, not noted for its entrepreneurial flair, was already the largest landowner in Spain. Generations of pious benefactions had already diverted much of Spain's wealth into a rural economy without economic "multipliers." Even before the riches of the Indies poured into silver chalices, golden retablos, cloth-of-gold vestments, and vast clerical estates, the proportion of Spanish wealth available for venture capital was diminishing.

The Church resisted change of any sort. The Inquisition was an anticapitalist as well as an anti-Protestant device. And, as the imperial period relapsed into exhaustion and cynicism, the Inquisition became anti-intellectual, and therefore antiscientific as well.

During the same period the thriving Spanish mercantile and banking system of the late Middle Ages suffered a blow to which it had been exposed more than any other country in Europe. The Christian kingdoms of the north provided exercise, booty, and endorsement of an economy of pillage to their more muscular subjects in their "reconquest" of the Moorish kingdoms. Meanwhile, the Black Death cut the peaceful labor force by a third or more. Mercantile Catalonia lost nearly half its population; these losses were especially severe among artisans, shopkeepers, and merchants. Barcelona's banks seem to have been peculiarly vulnerable, and many of them failed. Thereupon the kings turned to Genoa and then to Antwerp to finance their ambitions.

41

The windmills of La Mancha, home of impoverished but haughty sheepherders.

Soon afterward, silver and gold appeared from America. The Spanish economy provided no adequate channels into which this liquidity could be poured. Spain did not have the English habit of reinvestment. A sort of economic thrombosis ensued. The Genoese bankers were ready to help, and it is likely that they made off with at least a third of the swag.

The endless, fruitless Hapsburg wars were under way, so expensive that they would bankrupt any sovereign, no matter how rich in American booty. Debts had to be paid, crusades and dynastic bickers mounted and replenished. The loot of the Indies, Mexico, and Peru did not long remain in Spain. Shrewd Genoese, Flemings, and rising German bankers, chiefly the Fuggers, scooped in the gold and silver of the Incas and Aztecs.

The Spanish economy, hobbled to a Church resistant to money-lending at interest, could not digest sudden, unpredictable infusions of precious metals. Bold spirits were drawn to heroic overseas conquests, not to economic venturing at home; labor costs in Spain rose in part because escape to the colonies was available to those who survived the Plague. As Spanish and Portuguese inflation raged, the cost of manufacture in Castile and Catalonia rose far more rapidly than it did elsewhere in Europe. In distant Germany and Italy the impact of sudden silver was moderated by distance. Laborers in the inland countries had fewer alternatives than those on the Atlantic seaboard. Spanish manufacturers were ruined by Spanish riches; foreign competitors moved into their markets, creating a habit of foreign buying that persists to this day. (An analogue might be the propensity of American consumers of the 1980s to dampen the recovery of their own economy by their failure to invest and their lust for foreign-produced baubles and toys.)

The bourgeoisie of Spain, so gleeful and prosperous as the Age of Discovery opened, were desolated at its close. Like many Americans who acquire large sums of money from indulgent parents, they took shelter in the mores of the closest social anachronism. In Spain that was the code of the hidalgos, made even more thrombotic by the mesta's cozy aversion to competition.

In the Spanish countryside, which sent forth most of the impoverished but haughty horsemen who became conquistadors, there existed an institution without parallel in the English colonies: the mesta, a kind of producer cooperative developed by Christian sheep ranchers leasing land from Muslim lords. The mesta regulated pasturage by common consent and made it possible to have roundups followed by seasonal sheep and cattle drives. These may seem to us like rehearsals for the style of the American West, but the mesta was more of a guild than an American-style alliance of independent cattle barons. Putting the term "cattle kingdom" in quotation marks is a useful warning, however, against romantic visions of a life on the range independent of the commerical world, whether in nineteenth-century Wyoming or fifteenth-century Spain. Both systems sold their products into world markets; the countinghouses of the wool markets of Flanders were essential to the mesta, in much the same way that a railroad to Chicago made Dodge City possible. Without steak-eating cities there would have been no "cattle kingdoms." Merino wool without textile plants, however small in scale, is good for nothing but to warm a herd of starving sheep. The Jewish and Genoese merchants of the cities of Castile kept the Spanish economy in contact with the textile markets of Flanders and Catalonia, while Barcelona haggled with the Levant.

After the Black Death weakened the will of Spanish commerce and reduced the numbers of Spanish artisans and merchants, the sheep-driving magnates seized the moment to enlarge their role in the economy and in the nation's governance. The value of their landholdings was permitted by royal decree to rise with inflation while wages and mercantile profits were frozen by royal price and wage controls.

Two or three percent of the population owned ninety-seven percent of the land; the recalcitrant clergy, taken as a whole, was the richest class of all. The Crown was persuaded to assign to sheep-grazing — forever — all land upon which sheep had been grazed. For these reasons, Spain could not accommodate itself to the rise of a market economy, and industrialism came little and late.

I have mentioned Hapsburg wars and dynastic bickers. Seldom fought for reasons connected to the interests of the Spanish people or the Spanish economy, they were often disastrous for Spain. These disasters accelerated after the abandonment of the Holy League with England, which had been contrived at precisely the moment when Spain, in the fullness of crusading energy, exploded in the direction of the Americas. These two seafaring nations between them might have divided the world, leaving only the scraps to Portugal. But suddenly John, the only son of Ferdinand and Isabella, died. This was, as Walter Alison Phillips wrote in 1911, the "worst misfortune which ever happened to Spain." The desolated parents were forced to turn to the son of their insane daughter, Juana. Charles of Hapsburg became king, and "from that day Spain became a part — the leader, then the paymaster, then the dupe — of the international monarchical confederation called 'the illustrious house of Austria.'"

The Hapsburg dynasty depended on religious unity to hold together its sprawl of discontiguous fiefdoms from Hungary to Gibraltar and beyond. Religious unity required the expenditure of Spanish blood and four times as much revenue as Spain ever received from her American colonies. The Thirty Years War, fought for dynastic interests, devastated Germany and impoverished Spain. In providing garrisons for the line of communication between the Hapsburg possessions in Austria and those in the Netherlands, Spain's troop movements infuriated France. Wars fought to hold the Burgundian possessions in Flanders turned England, trading partner of the Dutch and Flemings, into Spain's implacable enemy, ready to assist in every way the rebellious provinces that became the Dutch Republic. The Hapsburg insistence upon the other pretensions of Burgundy, in the Jura, brought Spain into conflict with Geneva, the third emergent dynamo of capitalism in Europe, which was gaining wattage at a steady, if unglamorous, pace.

All the while, Spain's fleets were engaged in a perpetual conflict with the Turks in the Mediterranean, as the Ottomans ground their remorseless way up the Balkan peninsula toward the Hapsburg capital of Vienna.

Religious differences, of course, played a large part in this. The Dutch, Swiss, and English were predominantly Protestant. However, in the sixteenth and seventeenth centuries, while the missions were being financed with whatever the embattled Hapsburgs could spare, European statecraft could almost be explained *without* the Reformation. That long-delayed explosion did provide additional battle cries and new reasons for Protestants and Catholics to massacre each other. But reasons enough could be found in the dynastic interests of their employers and overlords.

Where religion mattered most was in America. There only avarice shared the affections of mankind with evangelical zeal. Only rarely (as we will observe in Florida and California) did religion have to compete with both avarice and dynastic ambition. In Europe it was otherwise.

Spain, having exhausted itself in crusading conflicts from the Aegean to the Strait of Magellan, isolated intellectually and drained of the *benefits* of imperialism, did not enter the modern world with sprightliness. The enemies of Spain embraced market-distributed economies, the factory system, the law of contract, and economic abstractions written on negotiable instruments. They reinvested wealth in further production. Ranged against Spain were the Dutch, the Swiss, the Jews (after Isabella piously exiled those she could identify), the Arab traders, and the English. If the last did not exactly fit Napoleon's description of "a nation of shopkeepers," their sovereigns and nobles, from Elizabeth onward, were an aristocracy of capitalists.

As Spain withdrew into its ancient self, it sent off to America its most energetic sons in alliance with those Hapsburg subjects from their other fiefs who could not accept what Europe was becoming. In the New World, some of them attempted to recreate, especially in the missions, what Europe had been but would be no more.

La Purísima Concepción de Nuestra Señora de Caborca.

45

Looking across the roof of San Ignacio de Caburica, Sonora,
from the bell tower to one of the domes.

THE MEDIEVAL CHURCH IN THE NEW WORLD

Spain invaded America at a time when the rest of Europe was making the transition from the world of *caballeros* and knights-errant, of the Black Prince and Cortés, of Hotspur, Pizarro, and de Soto, to the world of the Cecils and Fuggers, of Mazarin, Richelieu, and Necker, and, ultimately, of the Barings and Rothschilds. Spain decanted the Middle Ages into America. When America returned the spoils of empire, Spain knew no better than to take the money and buy more merino sheep, more palaces, and more vestments.

And more missions. At least four hundred in Mexico alone, and another hundred on the northern frontier. Medieval, Catholic Europe reappeared in the New World with no Reformation to distract it. No religious civil wars shattered the old order, as they did in France, where the Catholic aristocracy waded through Protestant blood toward a brief eighteenth-century quiet, and then into bloodier revolution. England decapitated kings, nobles, and bishops for their beliefs or for what others believed their beliefs to be. After these events, nothing was the same, but in Spain and Spanish America, bloodshed did not transform the old order. It merely extended it.

Remarkably, however, there did not arise in the New World either a feudal aristocracy or the sort of territorial grandees who emerged after feudalism to become the Whigs in England and the great nobility of France and Spain. The Cortés family and the Pizarros returned to Spain to buy land and sheep and to embrace again the world of the late Middle Ages. They became new faces in an old frame. In the early years of the reign of Charles V, the Cortés family reinvested its Mexican plunder in enough Spanish land to justify a marquisate (del Valle) and an income of 60,000 ducats a year, more than that of the ancient families of Alba or Medina-Sidonia (at a time when a laborer's annual income might be 20 ducats).

In New Spain the Crown and the Church prevailed. Agents of the Crown, viceroys and governors and *alcaldes*, vied with agents of the Church. But there was no vigorous merchant class to play Church against state, and no aristocracy with which to form alliances. This was a New World more like the Old World of the Middle Ages than the new world rising in Europe itself.

In New Mexico, after assassinating or expelling several governors and sending off another in chains, to die in a prison of the Inquisition, the Franciscans were able to establish a theocratic state quite independent of agents of the Crown. That state failed to account for the feelings of its subject-parishioners and thus collapsed in the Pueblo Revolt of 1680.

The struggle between state and Church was resolved in stages, commencing with the expulsion of the Jesuits by the king-emperor of Spain in 1767. A series of anticlerical revolutions erupted in Mexico during the nineteenth century. Finally, Texas, Arizona, New Mexico, and California were conquered by Americans, who, by any European standard, could be said to be anticlerical as well.

WAS IT A SPANISH EMPIRE?

Spain was no more a single unit than were the Spaniards a single people. Nor was what we have come to call "the Spanish Empire" only a Spanish undertaking. It was the reestablishment of Catholic Europe in a new arena.

The conquest and colonization of Mexico and Mesoamerica, Latin America, of an empire in North America reaching, at its most extended, to Lake of the Woods, Minnesota, and nearly to Savannah, Georgia, was, it is true, predominantly the work of people born in Spain. By no means, however, were the Spaniards alone in this amazing work.

"Spanish" Arizona, for example, was created by people serving the pope first and the Hapsburg dynasty second. Faith was compatible with fealty. It happened that Charles of Ghent (1500–1558) became Holy Roman emperor (Charles V) and sword of the pope. He was also heir to the fertile dukedom of Burgundy, which included Flanders and which produced a prodigious number of talented architects who would work in his American possessions. In Spain itself, arrogant Flemings arrived in the entourage of their new king in 1518, as Juan de Grijalva was reconnoitering the coast of Mexico for Cortés. Charles's Flemish courtiers were resented by the grandees of Spain, especially after they were given royal licenses to procure and sell Negro slaves in America and lucrative religious offices such as the archbishopric of Toledo, which went to Charles's sixteen-year-old nephew, Guillaume de Croy. Thereafter, as a new crop of Spanish aristocrats was being planted in America, the old ones at home, infuriated by the rapacious cosmopolitans surrounding Charles, refused him the title of "Majesty," which they reserved for his Spanish mother. They called him merely "Your Highness." The Franciscan who led the teaching and mission-building friars into Mexico was Peter of Ghent, the first of many of his countrymen. A century later the kings of Spain made an attempt to crop out non-Spaniards from the missionary field, so there was a sudden rush of renamings. A Jesuit named Van der Veken in Sinaloa became Del Rio, and Father Vandersnipe gained a new Christian name, Diego. (Michael Wading, an Irish Jesuit, accepted a complete repackaging as Miguel Godinez.)

The Franciscan order was established in the thirteenth century, *before* Europe entered the age of nationalism. The Jesuits emerged as a multinational order three centuries later, in the teeth of that nationalism, as instruments of the Counter Reformation. The Jesuit soldiers of the Church, organized along military lines, had a high regard for the workings of the human intellect and for systems organized by intellect. The modest adjustments of priestly names made by Jesuits serving Spain did not distract Spanish kings from the knowledge that many other Black Robes were serving France. Others would surely have served a Catholic king of England had the Stuarts prevailed. Nationalism could no longer brook such ambiguities, as the Jesuit martyrs to Spanish nationalism learned to their sorrow when they were expelled in 1767. Four centuries earlier, Charles of Ghent's Hapsburg ancestors lost most of their alpine lands to the peasants, led (we are told) by William Tell, but they retained some of their fiefs, now in Italy. From there came the most famous of the founders of Arizona, Father Eusebio Francisco Kino.

Though Kino and other clerical cosmopolitans were present in early Arizona and California, from a military and administrative point of view, Arizona was a Basque province. In the eighteenth century, Basques held the outposts of Arizona; a few left their progeny there, to be joined in the twentieth century by more Basques, who are often discovered today in shops and playing their own music to their sheep on mountain hillsides. The rough Basque country had been training frontier entrepreneurs for centuries; the famous first families of Arizona, the Anzas, Urreas, and Velderrains, were of Basque, not Castilian or Aragonese, descent. Why is this distinction important? Because the Basques were, in appearance, language, and custom, the ultimate expression of Spanish diversity.

In Arizona, Argentina, or their own homeland on the northeastern coast of Spain, traditional Basques do not call themselves by that name. They are Euskadi. Their language (Euskera) bears some relationship to Finnish and Hungarian and none at all to Spanish or to French. Their earliest inscriptions made use of letter-forms like those of the Levant, though the people were said by the twelfth-century Codex Calixtinus to be fairer in complexion than the neighboring Navarrese. Perhaps this may be explained in part by the fact that they were traders not only with the Moors but also with England and Ireland.

ITALIAN AND GERMAN ENGINEERS AND WILD GEESE

In the sixteenth century the now hostile English, singing new Protestant battle hymns, stormed ashore in the West Indies to capture the depots where the Spaniards had stored the plunder taken from America. Returning with their swag, Sir Francis Drake and Sir John Hawkins then prowled the coasts in search of vulnerable treasure-laden galleons. "Pieces [pesos] of eight!"

Drake pillaged Santo Domingo in 1585; Drake and Hawkins brought home to Queen Elizabeth a succession of luxuriant hauls from the Catholic silver fleets and coastal towns. In the terms used by modern economists, *not* getting the treasure home to Spain was an "opportunity lost cost." To diminish that loss, it became cost-effective for Spain to erect in America a system of fortress bases. The Spaniards — perhaps one should still say the Hapsburgs — responded by enlisting military engineers from their other dominions.

Italians, trained in Renaissance science, were important to the Catholic sovereigns, especially after the exile of skilled Arab and Moorish Muslims. Columbus, one of those scientific Italians, failed to find much gold in the first place he landed; his career sputtered out before the treasures of Peru and Mexico were looted by the next generation of conquistadors. Then the task of protecting the loot was given to another Italian, Bautista Antonelli, a military engineer. The magnificent fortifications still to be seen at Havana, Cuba; Cartagena, Colombia; Portobelo, Panama; Veracruz, Mexico; and St. Augustine, Florida, owe their origin to Antonelli, who began the work in 1581.

Nearly two hundred years later, the threat that the English might invade Mexico overland by way of Texas led Charles III, the last Bourbon king of Spain, to send Gaetano Maria Pignatelli Rubi Corbera y San Climent (a nobleman as Italian as Spanish) to reassess the northern defenses of the silver mines themselves, in Mexico. Those mines had a resurgence of production in the eighteenth century, but they were no longer easy to exploit simply by deploying battalions of Indians to work and die there. In 1786 Fausto d'Elhuyar y de Suvisa, director general of the mines in New Spain, and Thaddeus von Nordenflicht led teams of Germans to modernize and partially mechanize these operations. They established the first school of mines in the Americas.

The Marques de Rubi (as Pignatelli Rubi is generally known) selected Hugh (Don Hugo) O'Connor, late of Ireland, as first inspector-general of those defenses. Both were to serve under the viceroy, Don Antonio Maria Bucareli y Ursúa, another Italo-Hispanic, who succeeded a Franco-Hispanic, Don Francisco (Francois) de Croix, and was succeeded by Don Francisco's nephew Theodore (Teodoro). This Franco-Italian-Irish-Spanish syndicate reexamined the placement of the presidios which had occurred in 1752 at the command of Basques advised by Germans.

O'Connor was one of the "wild geese," the Catholic Irish gentry whose fathers or grandfathers had fled to Spain and France after failed risings against the British. The *alcalde* of West Florida was another O'Connor, John (Don Juan); Arthur O'Neil was its governor, and the "Spanish" governor of Louisiana in the 1760s was named O'Reilly. With all these broguish Spaniards about, and all the German Jesuits we will later pursue from Baja California to Arizona, it is obvious that what has been called "Spanish" colonial architecture was something considerably more complicated than that.

The fortress at Cartagena, Colombia, guarding the port city of the galleons.

The church of Cholula, under the volcano of Popocatépetl, near
Puebla, Mexico.

PART III THE ARCHITECTURAL MISSION

THE MEDITERRANEAN CONTRIBUTION

ON IBERIA'S BEACHES TODAY, blond tourists baste themselves, slumbering in the sun. In 1493 those beaches were as busy as those of Normandy in 1944, though the traffic was going toward the sea, not the shore. Embarkation for the Crusade upon America was under way (disembarkation from America, General Eisenhower's "Crusade for Europe," had to wait for 451 years.)

Queen Isabella was intent upon sending Catholic Europe on a new Crusade to Palestine, but she consented to send one first westward, having been assured that enough gold could be found in that direction to mount properly a later assault against Islam. So a stream of ships sailed westward, propelled by the urgencies of faith and of avarice. (Most of Isabella's vessels were smaller than the landing craft of 1944.)

Iberia was the spear of Catholic Europe, thrusting out into the Atlantic world. The pageant of conquistadors and friars, of caravels, galleons, and flotas, of Columbus, Pizarro, Cortés, and Coronado, so fills our imagination that it is difficult to recover the sense of what the peculiar geography of the western end of the Mediterranean meant for the *content* of conquest.

The invaders from Iberia bore with them memories of the world they were leaving behind, a world they were intent upon crystallizing anew in America. These Catholics were not merely going upon a mission of conversion; that might have been accomplished without conquest, as it had in Scandinavia and Ireland. They were determined to reconstitute in America the world of the western Mediterranean, which was as much North African as it was European.

This is a fact of some importance, apparent in outcomes and in origins, in the architecture they built when they came to America, but also by a simple glance at a map of their points of embarkation. At the Strait of Gibraltar, North Africa is as close to Spain as Martha's Vineyard is to Wood's Hole, and considerably closer than Catalina Island is to Long Beach and Los Angeles. The strait was not a barrier but a highway; culture had flowed across it for a millennium, drawing southern Spain into a cat's cradle of North African interests. Towns and buildings along the two shores were virtually indistinguishable from each other.

Catholic Europe meets Muslim Africa at Gibraltar and Tangier. The last vestiges of Islamic expansion in the Iberian peninsula were arrested by the "reconquest" of Granada under Ferdinand and Isabella, but a reconquest is not the same as a replacement. The people and architecture of Spain remained as they had been.

For seven centuries most of the energy in the Mediterranean basin had been Muslim, not Christian. In Spain, this Muslim energy went beyond the sort of military occupation that the Visigoths had imposed upon the rubble left by the collapse of the Roman Imperium. Muslim culture germinated and blossomed with equal vigor on both sides of the narrow sea lane uniting North Africa and Europe. Artistic developments flowed in both directions, but first from the cultivated south, bearing Byzantine, Iranian, Egyptian, and North African accomplishments into Spain. Then, after 1050, the balance of artistic influence tipped in the other direction, from the

north back to Africa. The Iberian peninsula and western North Africa were politically united by the Almorands and Almohads, the Berber dynasties that imported the lessons of Muslim Spain to their capitals in Morocco.

While the Crusaders were bringing Muslim learning back from the Levant to northern Europe, Muslim culture was also seeping northward into the Christian courts of Spain and across the Pyrenees into Aquitaine and the Auvergne in southern France. There it played a central role in creating the world of the troubadors and courtly love. (Arabs say that the word "troubador" comes from the Arabic verb *taraba*, to sing; Latinists prefer to believe it arose from the Latin word for composition.)

The importance of the Muslim southern shore to the Christian northern shore has recently been brought once again to mind by the delicious possibility that the Leaning Tower of Pisa, symbol of the onset of the Renaissance in Italy, may have begun its architectural career as a recollection of the minaret of the city of al-'Abbasiyya in Tunisia. Something very much like that minaret was described by the Arab chronicler al-Bakri before it was pillaged by the Pisans on their expeditions against "Ifriqiyya" between 1148 and 1160. The idea of a purloined minaret re-erected on amateurish (by Muslim standards) foundations on the Camposanto in Pisa in 1174 is delightful, but it is more likely that the tower represents a due respect for a higher culture. This thought is strengthened by the uncontestable presence in Pisa's cathedral of columns from the mosque of Mahdia. In Muslim Spain, Europe had found its schoolroom. Ibn Rushd, known in the West as Averroës, born in Córdoba in 1126, taught it algebra. Maimonides, a Jew, instructed about a new medicine grounded in scholarship in the old. Anesthetics were used and cataract operations performed. Spherical geometry was developed, scientific agriculture flourished, geography and astronomy provided the groundwork for the Age of Discovery. Arab navigation was more skillful than anything the Christians could muster, and the Arabs excelled in chemistry, physics, botany, and knowledge of the classics.

After this great civilization had been in place for seven centuries, its elite was replaced by a Christian one, but the people who had kept the culture alive did not disappear. Some continued to work in Spain, and many went on to America, still plying their crafts and imbued with their science.

There are lessons to be learned in the streets of Spain and Mexico. There, around the corner, is the sound of a lute (from Arabic *al'ud*) and an oval guitar. As they sound, a boy sings in the Arabic intonation that distinguishes Spanish music from that of Europe north of the Pyrenees. The Arabs brought to Spain new sounds, and they brought new crops — cotton, sugar cane, rice, palm trees, mulberry trees for silkworms to eat. They taught Europe how to irrigate these crops using water wheels. (The Hohokam in Arizona irrigated their cotton fields long before any Europeans came to America, and when the Spaniards brought to Arizona the technology they had inherited from Islamic Spain, they used the Hohokam ditches and cotton fields.)

By the eleventh century, Muslims had created one of the Old World's most subtle and elegant civilizations. The Renaissance did not occur in Muslim Spain or North Africa because no rebirth was necessary. Muslim tradition was continuous during the Carolingian Renaissance, Ottonian Renaissance, proto-Renaissance, and the Romanesque and Gothic periods.

The Casbah of Tiffoultoute in Morocco.

The culture of the Muslim Mediterranean was a powerful influence upon the architecture of the Spanish missions in America during the first great building campaign after the conquest. That is why the first Spanish churches created in America look so much like the small mosques of Algeria and Morocco. The churches built by Columbus at La Isabela and by his son Diego at Puerto Real had towers that, in another context, could have been minarets. Tourists from Tunis or Cairo may feel quite at home in the great cloistered complexes in Mexico; only a little more empathy is required of them in the smaller missions from California to Texas.

Islamic architecture, sustaining the lessons of the ancients into the modern age, was as important to the architecture of the American missions as the sputtering and awkward European revivals of learning and craftsmanship. While the terms Romanesque and Gothic may have some significance as applied to forms in northern Europe, even there they did not come in neat sequence. The two styles were contemporary, though the revival of round-arched, massive Roman forms commenced somewhat earlier and in more places than the pointed-arched Gothic form, with its increasing emphasis upon light and height. In Spain and its colonies, the two styles *remained* contemporaries until both were gradually fused into that second set of renewed Romanesque forms we call the Renaissance.

In California we find round-arched colonnades in the Roman fashion in three dimensions (as at San Juan Capistrano) and stylized in murals in two (as in the now whitewashed sanctuary at Pala). These colonnades might be Roman or Romanesque. If Romanesque, they might descend from North Africa or from Cluny (see p. 60). They might be from the second Romanesque, or Renaissance, transmitted directly from Spain or mediated by way of Mexico. In any case they are evidence of a very long progression from the Mediterranean to the Pacific.

From the fourth century through the fourteenth, North Africans built on a tradition inherited from Rome, reusing Roman masonry, setting up columns and giving them new capitals, reoccupying Roman towns, tuckpointing Roman brickwork, remilitarizing Roman forts, and rereading Roman treatises. The North African "Romanesque" and "Renaissance" had begun shortly after they toppled those columns and replaced Roman bureaucrats with their own. Then they set about creating architecture on their own.

In Spain the same process of replacement occurred in the three centuries between the withdrawal of the Romans and the appearance of Islam. Thereafter the polyglot people of the Iberian peninsula effected a new synthesis. Heirs to North African culture, they were also the frontiersmen of Catholic Europe and custodians of the even older decorative traditions of the Celtic north, which were as important in Galicia as in Ireland or Wales or Brittany. This composite they shipped to America.

Those who built the missions drew upon that composite, but not in the pedantic sense of imitating particular Islamic buildings, either observed or known from literary description. (Very little real architecture is created in accordance with the influence chasing of architectural history, except by architects who also teach architectural history and enjoy in-jokes.) Instead the mission builders recrystallized the elements they had experienced and installed in their memories. They drew upon a shared body of knowledge, much of it from the traditions of the southern Mediterranean. In a few cases their ornament or the rough shaping of facades was taken from books, and they were given rather vague directions from Madrid or their Mexican motherhouses as to the relationship of the parts to the whole mission complex.

But these builders were practical people meeting problems of construction and serving symbolic needs; they were not builders of theme parks, so we should not look to the missions for "tags" or "labels" to lead us back to prototypes. What we will find, instead, is the accumulation of a millennium of experience, transported and altered by circumstance. It is of crucial importance, however, that we not limit our expectations of what that experience produced to what we might find in northern Europe or in Christian Europe alone.

Mutations occurred. Creative people made new things, as the body makes new genes. But the mission-building process, like that of human reproduction, carried tens of thousands of already created forms and processes out of the past along with each new creation.

Once in America, these Afro-European eclectics acquired new ideas about the engineering of construction and about the art of ornament from the Native Americans, and created a repertory of building devices by which they carried out Europe's mission in America.

As ways of keeping students awake in class, these terms may be useful. But they may mislead the hasty into believing that what was appearing in Santo Domingo or Mexico City or later in Texas came in some Gothic-on-the-shoulders-of-Romanesque, Mozart-Haydn-Beethoven sequence, or that these forms emerged from the artistic crucible centering upon the North Sea instead of from the Mediterranean. In fact, the wonderful Romanesque cloisters of Mexico *and* its dozen of churches with Gothic elements are all products of the same culture of the Middle Ages, whether derived from Flanders or from the Mediterranean. The European style was modified by the taste and experience of Indians who already had an architectural tradition as ambitious and vigorous as anything in Europe or Africa. During the great campaign of mission construction in the mid-sixteenth century, hundreds of cloisters and churches were constructed by Franciscans, Dominicans, and Augustinians throughout central Mexico, along with a score of others in Yucatán and as many in the islands.

When we come upon the ruined nave of the basilica of the Dominican monastery at Cuilapán, in the state of Oaxaca, we might easily imagine ourselves in some forgotten valley in Wales. Here in the mist are the full arcades of a style that in the British Isles would be called "Norman." Only after the Norman invasion of 1066 were there builders capable of producing something so grand and solemn. In Mexico, as the mist rises with the sun, we are reminded that only after 1066 did Normans, whether in Britain or in Sicily, build the way Arabs had been building in dry Africa for the preceding three centuries. Cuilapán is Romanesque — that is to say, it is a product of that burst of opulence and energy which enabled Europeans after 1066 to emulate Roman architecture of the classical period. They might have built that way earlier, but they were too poor and distracted by civil broils and invasions to do so.

From the beginning of the second millennium onward, the Romanesque, whether in North Africa, Britain, or Spain, was the tradition to which conservative people turned. The Gothic was "modern," as its twelfth-century proponents proclaimed, though it held that uncontested title only for a brief time until it was challenged by the fresh revivals we describe as Renaissance. Sixteenth-century Spanish architecture in the New World partook of both modernities. At the extremities of the Catholic empire, Gothic modernism continued to commend itself to Catholic churchmen well

Above: Arches and columns in a patio of the Alhambra, Granada, Spain.

ROUND ARCHES

On the islands of the West Indies and on the mainland, in Yucatán and in Mexico, round arches, barrel vaults, and thick walls, built by Indians under the direction of Flemish, Italian, or Spanish architects working for kings of Spain, began to diverge from their European models. Sometimes the results are described as "Indo-Romanesque." When Indian laborers produced buildings with pointed arches and vaulting, soaring a little higher than that round-arched style, the result is sometimes called "Indo-Gothic."

into the nineteenth century. It was mixed, in what was called the "Plateresque" style, with Renaissance ideas — that is to say, with a more modern modernism, which was, in truth, a revival of the art of the ancients, and therefore more backward-looking.

There are many splendid Romanesque buildings in Mexico, including the Dominican monastery at Amecameca, in the state of México; the arcades of the Franciscan monastery at Izamal, in Yucatán, and of the Augustinian monastery at Acolman, in México; and the cloister of the Dominican monastery at Coixtlahuaca, in Oaxaca.

European prototypes come to mind, as do others along the southern shores of the Mediterranean crucible. Round-arched arcades of cloisters can be seen, though only in remnants, at the Great Mosque of Cairo and in the first Great Mosque of Seville, founded in 859. There are Muslim Romanesque cloisters in the Great Mosques at Mahdia, Sousse, Monastir, and El Qayrawan, in Tunisia. Monastir is especially interesting because its attenuated columns and the ornamented intersections of columns and lintels (probably an eleventh-century remodeling or extension) anticipate Brunelleschi's Foundling Hospital in Florence, of the middle of the fifteenth century. Perhaps its unknown Muslim architect, rather than Brunelleschi, might be called "the Father of the Renaissance."

Romans in Morocco: Caracalla's Arch in Mauretania, A.D. 100–300.

Above: Early cloisters: the Ibn Tulun Mosque in Cairo, with spiral minaret.

Among the descendants of that "father" was the anonymous architect of the magnificent Hacienda San Antonio Matute, in Jalisco. Round-arched arcades can be seen again, though they are ruder, in the Dominicans' cloister at Amecameca (built 1547–1562), and they burst into full "Romanesque" magnificence in the Franciscans' open chapel at Tlalmanalco.

When attenuated columns such as those at Monastir began to appear in Mexico and Yucatán at the end of the sixteenth century, they often rose to arches with scalloped edges in the Moorish fashion. In Texas and California, a few cloisters are in the heavy "Syrian" Romanesque style. More are in the thinner, taller format that signals the onset of the Monastir-

Florentine style. Among the most beautiful of these arcades are those in California at San Juan Bautista, San Antonio de Padua, San Miguel Arcángel, Santa Inés (Solvang), Santa Bárbara, San Luis Rey de Francia, and San Juan Capistrano, and at what is left of Nuestra Señora de la Purísima Concepción in San Antonio, Texas.

In California it is difficult to sort out the genuine extensions of this tradition from "reconstructions" like that at Carmel (see p. 174). Nonetheless, with some imagination one can still summon the experience of the Mediterranean tradition asserted by Muslims and Catholic Spaniards and exported to New Spain in the sixteenth century.

THE GIFT OF SAINT HUGH

Before it departed from Cádiz, the Mediterranean tradition was joined by another, which became present in all the New World Romanesque, a faint breeze out of the Cluniac Middle Ages. It may still be felt under any round arch in the courtyard of San Juan Capistrano. The Spanish Romanesque was, one can argue, subsidized by the Cluniacs, just as the Cluniacs were unintentionally subsidized by the Moors through the protection money extorted by rapacious Spanish monarchs.

Let us follow the flow of funds: Before it was quarried for building materials during the French Revolution, the abbey church of Cluny was more splendid than the Saint Peter's Cathedral of the popes (the old one, which has been replaced by the present Baroque structure). Saint Hugh (1024–1109), abbot of Cluny and one of the shrewdest statesmen of Europe, exerted his subtle and pervasive influence on Spain from this huge and magnificent building, and from his palace next door. The abbot made and unmade kings, subsidized building campaigns, provided mercenaries for dynastic broils, and as a colleague and ally of the papacy reasserted the power of the See of Rome. In Iberia the clergy had been cut off from the rest of Europe, and liturgies had grown in their own way; Saint Hugh worked to bring them into conformity. (For theologians, and for those who follow the views of Carl Jung on the importance of the transformation symbolism of the Mass in the old Spanish rite, this is a matter of some interest. If we wish to know the ways of the earliest Christians, we are interested in what was lost when Cluniac churchmen reasserted the dominance of the Roman liturgy over the Spanish sees.)

The European Romanesque had its highest expression in the complex of palatial buildings surrounding the motherhouse of the Benedictines, which functioned as a sort of "order of Cluny"; scores of smaller churches, including many in Spain, were either inspired by the awesome example of the abbey church at Cluny or were initiated with subsidies drawn from that fountainhead. Cluny would have had much less influence without the gold dispensed by its agents. That gold came largely from the *cense*, donations from Castilian monarchs, who in turn received it as *parias* from the rulers of Islamic Spain. Between 1060 and 1200, Saint Hugh and other abbots of Cluny drew more revenue from the Christian kings of Spain than from their own lands.

Hugh of Cluny was a mighty prelate, but he was forever in need of money. Like Michelangelo's papal patron for the Sistine Chapel, he was a man of expensive tastes, including a taste for profusion in sculpture and mural painting, applied to Roman forms. It was this opulence that distinguished the Cluniac style from that of the simpler Cistercians and gained it the opprobrium of Saints Francis and Dominic two hundred years later.

The cost of much Cluniac magnificence was borne, at third hand, by the Muslim rulers of Zaragoza, Toledo, Seville, and Badajoz, who prudently preferred tribute to pillage. Perhaps it would be kinder to say that they saw no need for bloodshed when the alternative was merely to placate the importunate and muscular knights of Spain with a little of the Saharan gold those caliphs had in ample supply.

The glories of the churches built under the influence of the Romanesque-loving monks of Cluny are recalled (though, it must be said, in much simplified ways) when the swallows and the tourists come back to Capistrano. As one prowls California or Mexican cloisters in the scented evening, smelling musk and orange blossoms, sensing the sound of pious chanting just beyond the range of hearing, just beyond that may be a hint of the howls of emirs as they were squeezed for more bags of gold.

The Romanesque colonnade of San Juan Capistrano, California.

And that at San Miguel Arcángel, California.

FRANCISCAN GOTHIC

There were Goths in Spain, but they knew nothing of the "Gothic." Unless they were captured by Moors and carried off to Africa, they could never have seen pointed arches or buttresses. The Arabs and Berbers who came into Spain after them were more cultivated folk. They had known of the building forms we call Gothic for a thousand years. Pointed arches came out of the Middle East. First deployed by the Assyrians before 700 B.C., they were in use in Syria before the Muslim conquest. These arcades of pointed arches came into their fullest expression in the mosques of Cairo, beginning with that of Ibn Tulun in A.D. 876–879 (Ibn Tulun was trained at Samarra in Iraq).

The full panoply of "Gothic" arches, including the Tudor and the celebrated horseshoe arch we tend to call Moorish, was in use across North Africa on a grand scale before any appeared in Europe.

A tourist who wants to see good examples of the simple pointed arch made of sun-dried brick, as built by the Assyrians seven centuries before Christ and thereafter by North Africans, as taken up after 1000 by Spaniards and after 1525 by Mexicans, can look along the flanks of the Mission San José y San Miguel in San Antonio, Texas, or the mission church of Santa Bárbara, in California.

An old tradition in the New World: an unplastered adobe arch at the Dar Al-Islam Mosque, under construction in Abiquiu, New Mexico.

Rib vaulting, produced by linking a series of pointed arches, appeared in Europe soon after the first Crusaders returned from Syria and Palestine, where rib vaulting was in regular use. But for Americans and Mexicans, it is not Crusader Gothic but Franciscan Gothic that first comes to mind.

Francis of Assisi was a merchant who knew Islam. He preached in Egypt before the sultan himself, having sought and been accorded what was in effect ritual capture by the Muslims. Only a shipwreck deprived him of a later missionary visit to Islamic Spain. There are those who believe that he learned from Islam his emphasis upon a mendicant clergy. "Mendicant" means beggar. Orders of mendicants, such as the followers of Saint Francis or of his contemporary and friend Saint Dominic, and the Augustinians, espoused a life of simplicity and personal poverty. Their members had to abandon ownership of rich goods, leave their homes, and go into service, gaining their living by asking charity of others. These orders were organized on roughly egalitarian terms, though of course the human instinct for power and prominence could not be wholly eradicated — sainthood was not required of all. Saint Francis, though very well educated, regarded schooling and even literacy as incidental to the work of his disciples.

Immediately after his death in 1226, the followers of Francis began to build an immense pilgrimage church upon the escarpment above Assisi, so quickly did the human need to associate magnificent objects with magnificent spirit assert itself. His life and doctrine comment wryly upon the magnificence of the church bearing his name; nonetheless his example and its example have ever after gone out together into the world. Poor, begging friars, many of them illiterate by his injunction, have found shelter in monasteries swollen with the wealth poured upon the Franciscan order.

The upper church of San Francisco in Assisi, rendered transparent — one might say immaterial or insubstantial — to the faith by the frescoes of Cimabue and Giotto, set the model from which were derived, in humbler and simplified form, many of the missions built in America. The church was created in violent times, as were its successors. From the exterior it appears to be a fortress, its windows above the height of any ladder. Its turretlike buttresses, some with low flying arches, permit these walls to carry the weight of a cross-vaulted ceiling (two such ceilings, for both the upper and lower churches are vaulted).

There are no side aisles in the church of Saint Francis: it is a long, dark, shadowy, single space. There is neither transept (cross form) nor dome, even though domes were being built nearby; new cathedrals throughout northern Italy were being built on the many-domed Venetian-Byzantine model. Along the southern shore of the Mediterranean, from Syria to Spain, mosques were being remodeled and enlarged with domes. The Franciscans merely avoided such extravagances, at least then. As we shall see, only toward the end of their New World mission for Spain did they become converted to Jesuit opulence, most conspicuously in their use of Jesuit domes (see p. 90).

The first Franciscan church, dedicated to Saint Francis in his birthplace, Assisi, Italy, and for centuries the center of Franciscan mission activity.

Until then, straightforward basilicas with no aisles or domes were the rule in the Americas. Though cross-shaped churches, often with domes at the crossing, appeared in the eighteenth century, it is noteworthy that even the immense churches built before 1700 by the Franciscans, such as the four missions southeast of Albuquerque in the Salinas National Monument, at Awatovi among the Hopi, and the seventeenth-century church at Pecos — did not have transepts. They sometimes had rudimentary abutments in that direction, but these went all the way back to the bema, the raised platform around the altar reserved for the clergy, in the earliest Christian churches of Rome, such as the basilica of the old Saint Peter's.

Transepts and domed crossings were Jesuitical; even El Gran Convento, the Franciscans' headquarters in Mexico City, eschewed such extravagance. Even later, when transepts did appear in the plans of Franciscan churches, they were not used processionally, as if they were crossings; they merely contain subsidiary rooms. In adobe churches, which feel as if their spaces were hollowed *out* rather than built *around*, the walls containing these ancillary chambers feel like quarries from which just enough material has been removed to construct a sacristy or chapel. This is even true of the stone or brick churches of Arizona and New Mexico, which probably outnumbered those of adobe. There is not a single instance of a thin brick skin drawn tight across scaffolding. That came into the northeastern part of America from the Gothic of the North Sea region.

As our pages of floor plans demonstrate, the grand-slam Baroque cruciform plan was very rarely used in even the largest of the mission churches built by Spain within what is now the United States.

The mendicants did build large — larger than one might at first think, until one compares an apparently small church, such as that at Taos, New Mexico, with one, such as San Xavier del Bac in Arizona, whose volume, soaring in a dome and high-ceilinged transept leaves no doubt of its grandeur (surprisingly, the floor plan at Taos is 25 percent larger). Even if one looks only at the "footprints" on our pages of floor plans, remote and unpretentious San Antonio de Padua, in California, is nearly twice the size of San Xavier. No doubt it never *felt* that way; San Xavier is full of magic, and magic does not yield to measurement.

All authority proceeded from the center, Rome. There were a few Franciscan popes very early on, but the Jesuit order and the papacy were in symbiosis until political pressures by the Bourbon monarchs, besieging an aging pontiff at the end of the eighteenth century, forced their separation.

The Jesuits had earned a reputation for worldly cosmopolitanism, taking proper pride in Father Eusebio Kino. Though most of us associate Kino with the missions of the Pimería Alta, the Arizona-Sonora borderland, his geopolitical vision extended from Japan to Quebec. But the Jesuits were not alone in setting globe-girdling intellects to work in the New World. The Augustinians discovered the northeasterly course of the Japan current, and with it a safer route for the Manila treasure fleet, while the Carmelites secured the sources of vitamin C along the California coast that kept that fleet alive. (Carmel-by-the-Sea owes its origin not to golf but to scurvy; until fruits and vegetables were found there to give some protection from that mariner's curse, the brisk triangular trade from Acapulco to Manila and back again via the north Pacific was a healthful one.)

Those who feared the Jesuits as militant intellectuals in the service of the pope feared most their refusal to be penned within the borders of the rising new nation-states. The very name "Jesuits" was first uttered, in derision, by John Calvin, who saw them as the most redoubtable of his multinational opponents.

Despite the ultimate decision of their king, Charles III, to expel the Jesuits, the Spanish nobility has had a special affinity for the Society of Jesus, as it had earlier been drawn to the Dominicans, whose founder, Domingo de Guzmán, was born at Calaruega in Castile. The founder of the Jesuits, Iñigo de Oñaz y Loyola (Saint Ignatius of Loyola, 1491–1556) was a Basque nobleman who had served as a page at the court of Ferdinand and Isabella. Perhaps some of the nobility were aware that the king's expulsion of Jesuit intellectuals was no better way to build a lively culture than had been the expulsion of Moorish and Jewish intellectuals by his predecessors.

Opposite: Looking upward into the dome, lit by Moorish windows, of San Xavier del Bac. As the figures blur with age, it becomes easier to place this space and these surfaces in the traditions of both the northern and the southern shore of the Mediterranean.

AMERICAN GOTHIC

Though ecclesiastical politics were important in the Americas, politics having little to do with nationalism had architectural consequences. Let us bring this discussion down to a series of instances by recalling the first church of Saint Francis, in Assisi, and leaping from there to the first *American* church of Saint Francis, built by the Franciscan Peter of Ghent in Mexico City. We can only intuit its appearance, since little more of it remains than of the Aztec temple it replaced. We *do* know that Cortés supplied the money and an Aztec *teocalli* the building stone.

The gospel had first been preached on the American continent shortly after the year 1000, by priests brought along by Leif Ericsson. Five centuries later, in 1519, at Tlaxcala, four allied Indian kings were baptized, with Cortés and his lieutenant, Alvarado, as their godfathers. To mark that occasion, another church of San Francisco was built there soon after the conquest. It, too, was composed of reused Aztec stones. The Spaniards of that generation were capable of doing this with bluff self-assurance. Their ancestors had come down from their relatively barbaric uplands into the presence of one civilization, that of the Moors, whose architectural achievements were far larger than their own. Now, only a few years later, the Spaniards had clawed their way into the precincts of another high civilization.

Some of those who obliterated the great city of Tenochtitlán (Mexico City) and replaced it with their own version of a provincial Castilian town may have been present when Ferdinand and Isabella accepted the capitulation of Muslim Granada. Aztec Mexico was just another exotic field for pillaging — and for saving souls. So in Tenochtitlán and in Tlaxcala they were not abashed to reuse the masonry chiseled and polished by their betters, as they had often done in the Moorish kingdoms.

On Hispaniola, the island the Spaniards called Española, there were no Aztec stone temples and no Moorish foundations. The first Christian church in the hemisphere after the Viking shelters was built by Christopher Columbus at La Isabela, on the north coast of the island, in the mid-1490s. (It was not a mission but a garrison church.) Only ruins of this church remain, but it seems to have had Gothic touches; archaeologists working at the site of Columbus's son's settlement of 1504 at Puerto Real, a little farther along the north coast of Hispaniola, suggest that the stone gargoyles found there may have been transferred from the earlier church. Carved stone was even more worthy of reuse on Hispaniola than Roman or Muslim columns in Toledo had been.

The first cathedral of the Western Hemisphere was begun by Diego Columbus in 1512 in the city of Santo Domingo, and it took thirty years to construct. It is very grand, giving an appropriate sense of scale to the relatively tiny, muted Gothic Saint Luke's at Smithfield, Virginia, and other Virginia churches built more than a century later, including that more recently reconstructed at Jamestown.

The first hints of the dawn of the Renaissance appear at the west doorway of the Cathedral of Santo Domingo, which has pairs of classical double columns, though the north entry is thoroughly rooted in the Middle Ages, with pointed arches. The structure is Gothic, with a series of rib vaults, but already one can observe the Spanish propensity for intricate Gothic ornament upon a sober classical grid.

In Spain this combination was called Plateresque — in the style of silverwork. A somewhat similar style had appeared in the work of silversmiths working to supply the advanced taste of the Hapsburg regime of Charles V, grandson of Ferdinand and Isabella. It replaced the purer Gothic, which because she liked it is called "Isabelline."

It would probably be more useful to call the style Columbus left behind Gothic, to recall the Visigothic ancestors claimed by both Ferdinand and Isabella. Then the style of their successors, Diego Columbus, Cortés, and Charles V, might be "Hapsburg." That would remind us of Spain's forced participation in the Counter Reformation, which had Italian origins like those of the re-Romanizing of the Renaissance, after the death of Isabella in 1504.

Perhaps all that is of marginal interest to North Americans, for we have enough to digest in the profusion of Mexican Gothic without requiring that we sort out why or whether it might be Gothic, Isabelline, Plateresque, Hapsburg, or Renaissance. Therefore, after this detour back to the Columbuses and their island, we return to the Franciscans and to their church at Tlaxcala.

It is as flat-roofed as the first two churches, but, as we might expect of the Franciscans, the cloister has low, slightly pointed Gothic arches, and the floor plan is a reduced version of the church of Saint Francis at Assisi. Here, rather than in the squarer and more complex plan of the cathedral at Santo Domingo, is the prototype for hundreds of subsequent long, thin mendicant mission churches — aisleless, tall, and, when ambitious, terminating in a polygonal apse.

(The Augustinians tended toward a more elaborate Gothic, as demonstrated by their very early cloister at Yuririapundaro in the state of Guanajuato. Neither they nor the Dominicans built missions in what is now the United States.)

At Teposcolula, in the state of Oaxaca, the Dominicans created another form, a hall church centered upon a vaulted hexagonal space with a star formation somewhat like that of the wondrous Bohemian Gothic. Did a Czech Dominican wander all the way to Teposcolula even earlier than a Croatian Jesuit (see p. 115) explored California?

We can still visit many of these vaulted "Gothic" churches in Mexico. They appear to be fortresses, because their precursors in Europe often were, but few of them actually had that function. People who are engaged in sustaining a tradition often adopt familiar forms that have outgrown their function, thereby baffling archaeologists of a practical sort.

Most of these Mexican churches, and a few that are similar to them in the United States, have buttresses the full height of the walls, capped with battlements, with deep-set, splayed windows set safely high, where the trajectory of a musket ball or arrow could not reach the congregation.

For lovers of Gothic vaulting, the people who make pilgrimages to Gloucester Cathedral or to the tomb of Henry VII at Westminster Abbey, here is a list of some of the best of it to be found in Mexico:

Tepeaca, Puebla, Franciscan (1530–1560)
Cholula, Puebla, Franciscan (1549–1552)
Tula, Hidalgo, Franciscan (1550–1553)
Acolman, México, Augustinian (1539–1560)
Huejotzingo, Puebla, Franciscan (1529–1570)

Only at the Mission San Gabriel Arcángel in California, which today is beset by recording studios and used-car lots, did the Franciscans attempt Gothic vaulting within what is now the United States. That vaulted roof lasted only two years and was replaced by a flat one as a concession to the San Andreas Fault in 1807. But the church, despite its inelegant setting, has many other lessons to teach, including those imparted by subsequent earthquakes.

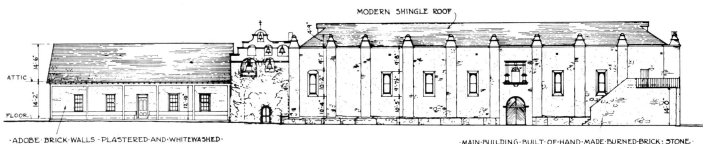

MODERN SHINGLE ROOF

ATTIC

FLOOR

·ADOBE·BRICK·WALLS·PLASTERED·AND·WHITEWASHED·

SOUTH ELEVATION

·MAIN·BUILDING·BUILT·OF·HAND·MADE·BURNED·BRICK; STONE·
·AND·LIME·MORTAR; COATED·WITH·THIN·PLASTER·
·SACRISTY·AND·BAPTISTRY·HAVE·MASONRY·VAULTED·ROOFS·
·MASONRY·VAULT·OVER·NAVE·HAS·BEEN·REPLACED·WITH·
·WOOD·ROOF·&·CEILING·

During the 1930s the Works Progress Administration financed the Historic American Buildings Survey (HABS) to record the appearance and dimensions of imperiled buildings and to jog Americans' sense of trusteeship.

67

RIBATS

We have noted the absence of stained glass images in the missions. The Gothic of Mexico and of the Mediterranean is not the sun-seeking Gothic of the north of Europe. Fortress cathedrals such as those at Albi, in southern France, and Palma, on Majorca, provide shelter from the unrelenting sun as well as protection from military attack. So do the churches of Mexico, New Mexico, and Texas, as the Alamo (San Antonio de Valero) demonstrated twice.

The Muslims inaugurated this tradition; guides to the cathedrals of Palma and Seville point out that they were built on Muslim foundations and on Muslim ecclesiastical-military principles. The south shore of the Mediterranean bristled with such buildings. The Muslims called them *ribats*.

The Arabs used arcaded courtyards to provide for the crowds of worshipers who assembled within the fortress walls of their ribats. The monastery courtyards of Spain and Latin America are like those within ribats as well. Sometimes they are on a grand scale, surrounded by refectories, chapels, hives of clerics and bureaucrats. Always there are courtyards and open chapels to contain processionals of the devout. In these interior courtyards, fountains splash and please, fruit trees and conversations blossom; one may smile because one feels secure. Monks or mullahs may stroll in shaded cloisters made musical by water and birds. There is a stout wall between all this and the hot, hostile, dry, and deadly world.

A ribat in Rabat, Morocco. The gateway into the casbah.

Sanctuary is holy safety, as much spiritual as military.
Saint Francis at Ranchos de Taos, New Mexico.

The Islamic world was lined with ribats — in Central Asia, along Saharan ridges, in the Spanish mountains to guard against Christian raiding parties, and along the coast where Vikings, indifferent to the religious inclinations of their victims, prowled in search of wealth unable to protect itself.

Many of these fortress mosques and fortress monasteries had towers; it was said that fire signals could be sent the 2,400 miles from Alexandria to Ceuta in a single night. Often such a signal tower was also a minaret.

These masonry walls were built in Chaco Canyon, New Mexico, about 925 in the Christian reckoning, while the Romanesque style was getting under way in Europe.

It is conventional to speak of the thick walls of New Mexican mission churches as having been determined by the traditions, and, it is even said, by the limited competence, of the Pueblo labor force. True, a thousand years of Pueblo architecture had gone into providing secure exterior walls; their Chacoan ancestors had demonstrated that what was made strong could also be made beautiful. But it is true as well that the churches at Trampas or Taos, New Mexico, look very much like mosques built in the Mediterranean in the tenth century, at the same time as the larger pueblos at Chaco Canyon.

The missions, unlike the pueblos and mosques, had bells and twin towers. These features came not from North Africa but from the monastic tradition of northern Europe. Still, many fortified missions along the Chichimac and Apache frontiers of northern Mexico sported only one signal tower. Their ruins today are quite indistinguishable from scores of ruined ribats along the frontiers of Islamic North Africa.

THE RIBAT ON THE SUNSET STRIP

The little mission of San Gabriel Arcángel once stood amid thriving wheat fields, producing the largest crops recorded for any mission in California. Now its location is given in the Los Angeles metropolitan telephone directory as 537 West Mission Drive. The wheat fields are gone, replaced by an asphalt desert.

The church walls are six feet thick, with buttresses capped with bristling crenelations similar to those atop the walls of innumerable examples of Islamic architecture, from the ribat at Sousse to the great mosque at Córdoba.

Father Cruzado, who was responsible for organizing the construction of San Gabriel, came from Córdoba, the birthplace of the Roman philosopher Seneca, the poet Lucan, Averroës, and Moses Maimonides. In Córdoba — city of leather, of gold from Ghana, and silver from the Sierra Morena — the making of paper and crystal glass and the casting of iron were perfected, and the Iraqi émigré Ziryab added a fifth string to the lute. Ziryab also defined Andalusian cuisine, conceived the toothbrush and toothpaste, and taught refined table manners.

In its heyday under the caliphs, Córdoba was probably the largest city of western Europe, with some 470 mosques and 300 public baths. The caliphal library held 400,000 volumes in the year 1000, while that of the famous Christian monastery of Ripoll had 192.

Father Cruzado came to Los Angeles from this fountainhead of learning, and he probably brought his toothbrush. He had grown to manhood in the presence of the majestic cathedral of Córdoba, the old great mosque transformed into a church. That building is so important in architectural history that one might call it the collection point of the European-African tradition. It is surely the ancestor of San Gabriel, for from Córdoba lines of force reach across the Atlantic to Mexico and the Spanish borderlands. At the ends of these lines stand many churches appearing to be fortresses, of which that at San Gabriel is the most startling because of its situation amid the asphalt, recording studios, flesh shops, strip joints, fast-food emporia, and car washes.

The Córdoba cathedral may be its prototype, but so might any number of fortress mosques. Some might think of the church of San Gabriel as a reduction, a miniature, of a larger fortress, such as those at Seville or Niebla, where the North African tradition is presented on a grand scale. Some might prefer to trace the church back to fortress cathedrals built to resist Muslim or Christian raiders — Albi or Palma. They manifest the same stern qualities — thick masonry walls with high windows and readily defended portals, buttresses crowned with merlons (battlements), behind which defenders may reload in relative safety while repelling attack.

Battlements appear atop many church walls in Mexico. They are most militant at the Augustinian monastery at Yecapixtla, in the state of Morelos, which has two battlemented towers drawn almost exactly from those of Seville. Though towers *might* house bells, there is no doubt that they were convenient for sharpshooting harquebusards and musketeers.

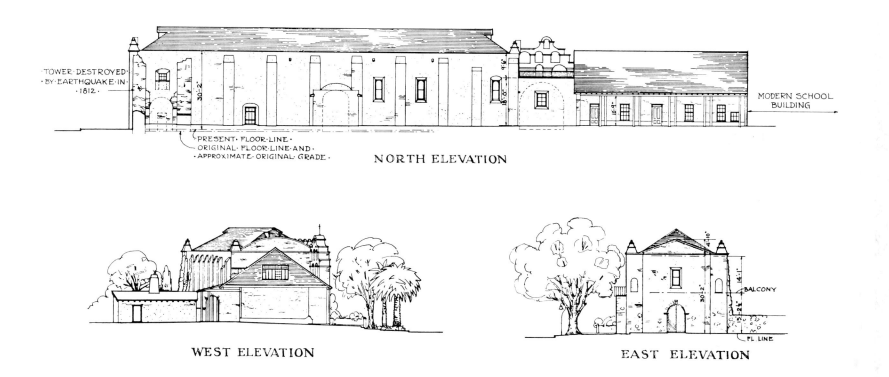

NORTH ELEVATION

WEST ELEVATION

EAST ELEVATION

This is a HABS drawing of San Gabriel Arcángel in Greater Los Angeles.

As the forces of Catholic Europe fought their way into Mexico and planted garrisons, they quickly demonstrated the efficiency of combining places of safety and places of worship. To this day, in remote places, these formidable churches remain, facing down any casual bandit who might presume to pillage. Solid, implacable apses confront the world; heavy wooden doors covered by gun ports open into antechambers where attackers may be compressed, surprised, and baffled.

The direct predecessors of the Franciscan San Gabriel in Alta California may be the Franciscan monasteries at Dzidzantun in Yucatán, or Tapeaca or Cauatinchan in Puebla, with their formidable buttresses, towerlike apses and battlements, or the Dominican monastery at Yanhuitlan in Oaxaca. San Gabriel has been plastered, somewhat smoothing its militancy, but the bald masonry of these Mexican churches frowns without even a hint of complacency.

THE HORIZONTALITY OF MOSQUES AND MISSIONS

The mission churches within the United States that still stand are too modest to display the most distinctive quality that the Spaniards derived from Muslim architecture: their great horizontal extent. The seven-aisled, mosquelike Capilla Real at Cholula in Mexico is the most dramatically Islamic structure built in the Western Hemisphere before oil-rich Arabs and Iranians began constructing genuine mosques in Washington and New York after World War II.

The open chapels of the Florida missions are all gone now; the English burned out their walls thoroughly. Even their locations have been lost. So these buildings, similar to those that assembled the followers of Mohammed in North Africa, are no longer available to remind us of this tradition. The horizontal church, therefore, is a form we no longer share with the traditions of Mexico and Yucatán.

There is a fundamental difference between the improvised, transitory, and deliberately impermanent brush arbors (of which we may be reminded each time we stop at a Ramada Inn) of the first missions and the brick and stone churches built both in Mexico and in what is now the United States in the next stage of permanency. And there is a difference between these and the adobe mission churches that also are found — though not, as we have seen, as frequently — in the American Southwest. Adobe crumbles and erodes. Stone does too, though not so quickly. Anyhow, it is not available in many places, and is more difficult to cut, to work, and to lay. In any case, the shape of a building constructed with adobe blocks, however buttressed, and with a few precious wooden beams carried long distances, is quite different from that of a stone building roofed with brick laid by vault-making craftsmen.

Though the wide church, roofed permanently, did not appear north of the Rio Grande, it is a conspicuous presence in Mexico. How did it develop? The followers of Islam do not often use a processional form of worship, nor did Islam's early evangelists in the Mediterranean require as much shelter from the cold as did the Calvinists of snowy Switzerland or the Knoxites amid the Scottish sleet. The message of Islam was often imparted out of doors, and so was the message of Catholic Christianity in the New World. Conditions around the Caribbean were not universally dry, but they were never very cold. In the islands, Florida, Yucatán, and Mexico walled or arcaded "open chapels" were common. They provided precedents for similar chapels in Arizona and New Mexico. There are, however, no direct descendants in the United States of the carefully designed courtyard churches of the Mediterranean, the West Indies, and Mexico. In the Southwest, services were indoors, with only an occasional sermon preached outside when there was an overflow crowd.

The wide National Cathedral in Mexico City.

The narrow interior of San Juan Capistrano in San Antonio, Texas.

The organization of the interior space, however, does owe something to Islam. The daily renewal of the Muslim faith occurs as each individual faces Mecca. This results in a multitude of units of worship, each the size of a rug, all facing in the same direction. But this direction does not converge upon the same point in every mosque building; the prayer rugs may not be aligned toward a lectern or even toward an altar. This multiplicity of worshiping modules is a matter of considerable interest to those who design mosques.

When a great mosque like Córdoba's La Mezquita was converted to Christian use, processions and preaching had to take place within a space that had been created to accommodate many rectangular rugs with people on them. Later, after 1402, this Muslim accommodation of elbow and knee room was emulated in the vast expanses of the Cathedral of Seville, the largest of medieval Europe. Though by no means the tallest, it is eight times the *width* of Westminster Abbey. That amplitude was established upon the

foundations of a mosque, whose minaret became the famous Giralda tower (emulated by Bertram Goodhue in the cluster of buildings for the Panama-California Exposition at the San Diego World's Fair of 1911–1915, which launched the Mission Revival of the 1920s).

Americans seeing for the first time the cathedrals of Santo Domingo and Mexico City (begun in 1553) are often struck by how wide they are. These are descendants not only of Spanish cathedrals but of the entire course of Mediterranean architecture of the seventh through the fifteenth centuries.

Among American mission churches only the Alamo gives the same impression of breadth. But perhaps that is because it was never completed; what we see now is an imaginative version of how the upper walls and roof might have looked, but without the intended dome, which would have made it seem less broad — "more like a church," as the expression goes.

Ceramic patterns in the Royal Baths at the Alhambra.

IN THE NEW WORLD

ON THE SURFACE

THE CLIFFLIKE, INSCRUTABLE exterior walls of the American missions were relieved by sculpture around their doors and windows and often by celebratory ornament on the front facade and bell towers. In Spain and in Mexico, painted decoration was augmented with colored and glazed tiles which, like well-shined shoes or a soldierly grin, did not diminish the military effectiveness of these buildings but did make them more ingratiating.

The Arabs encrusted surfaces with glazed tiles and stucco work that simulated tiles. The abstract patterns they used had much in common with the geometric ornament of the Aegean and with the Anasazi murals of the San Juan Valley of Colorado. Several of the Texas churches bear witness to this Muslim tradition of ornament, carried into Spain and on to Mexico.

It is often said that these Texas churches were covered with blue snowflake patterns. It is doubtful that the Franciscans who colonized Texas had much direct experience with snow, but they had ample contact with the magnificent tiled churches of Puebla and other Mexican training centers, which looked back toward the tile-making tradition of Moorish Spain.

Decorative painting was evident "everywhere on the entire [front] facade" of the Alamo, according to W. Eugene George, Jr., who scrutinized it for the Historic American Buildings Survey. According to a description of La Purísima Concepción, also in San Antonio, as it appeared in 1890, the building "must have been very gorgeous with color, for it was frescoed all over with red and blue quatrefoil crosses and with yellow and orange squares. . . . This frescoing is rapidly disappearing. . . . The baptistry walls are frescoed with weird-looking designs. Tops of side walls . . . have wide stone serration in the Moorish character." These buildings have since become sufficiently stark to placate Cotton Mather, but when they were new they must have been celebratory enough to please a Moor or a Spaniard or an Indian. In the 1770s Father Juan Agustin Morfi wrote of San José y San

Miguel that it was brilliantly polychromatic, its facade painted in yellow, red, blue, and black, its niches proud with painted statues of the saints. (San Francisco de la Espada and San Juan Capistrano were painted only on the inside and perhaps around the doors and windows.)

The California missions have also been bleached to an acquiescent coral color; their exterior sculpture, once brightly painted, and their interior walls have been whitewashed or even plastered to hide their intended vehemence. By 1920 they had become Bauhaus versions of what Walter Gropius might have designed for a mission, if all he could alter from the original plans was their color.

Painstaking research and restoration, much of it by Norman Neuerburg, have brought many of the missions back toward their original schemes. Neuerburg informs us that the original exuberance of color cannot be said to be the result of an unbroken sequence from the bright colors of the Indians of central Mexico. One can still see that color in the murals at Teotihuacán and upon the stones of each newly excavated Aztec or Mayan site.

The first missionaries recoiled from colors such as these, as they may have recoiled somewhat earlier from the decoration in the Moorish palaces of Granada. At Acolman, Actopan, and Huejotzingo they instituted a stark black-and-white mural tradition that was enormously powerful in its restraint; perhaps it was an anti-polychromy to go with their campaign against what they took to be barbarism. By the end of the sixteenth century, however, color returned. If friars scouted widely from their settlements in Baja California, they could scarcely have been unmoved by the immense murals on the cliff faces of the lower peninsula. In Alta California, there were freely decorated caves in the Chumash country around Santa Barbara. Did any of the friars see the giant intaglios near the present town of Blythe? One figure of a man is 167 feet tall and 164 feet from one outstretched hand to another.

The Muslim contribution to the ornamentation of mission churches is seldom emphasized; most of the discussion, especially in Mexico, has to do with the Indians' contribution of design ideas. Hot and dry climates the world over have produced similar architectural materials and design. But some variations in the play of geometry and fancy, some botanical motifs laid upon a trellis of abstract form, are peculiarly Muslim. Their tradition can be observed as it moved with succeeding generations out of the Middle East into Egypt, across North Africa to Spain, across the Atlantic to Mexico, and north into California, Arizona, and Texas. (Little of it can be seen in New Mexico because so little has survived, not because it was not there.)

Above: Mosaic tiles at the Alhambra.

The Indians, especially the Maya, had their own decorative twinings upon a grid. But no one would mistake them for the Muslim-Mediterranean-Mexican motifs now often denoted by the term "Mudéjar." In its precise use, Mudéjar means the art of a Muslim executed for a Christian patron, but it has come to mean any art or architecture which looks like that done in Spain by former subjects of the Moors — whether they themselves were Christians or Muslims — for a Christian client. That is how Kurt Baer, another student of the California missions, uses the term in writing about Carmel:

> The richest ornament and that most Moorish in feeling is at Mission San Carlos [Carmel]. Over the entrance door . . . is the . . . Mudéjar window, a star-shaped opening designed from the combination of the circle and square. . . . The framing of the arched door with its

concentric moldings . . . resembles the ancient Roman models. . . . The interior doorway to the side chapel . . . [has] smooth columns that suggest the Doric . . . [framing] a delicate Mudéjar arch.

There are many Moorish apertures to be found in the mission churches of San Antonio, Texas; the window known variously as the Rose Window (though it bears no relationship to Gothic rose windows) or Rosa's Window at San José y San Miguel is the most famous. It deserves a better fate than to be attributed to the influence of a mythical woman named Rosa. For if it be hers, how do we account for so many others like it in Cairo, Córdoba, and, indeed, in California?

The reach of Islam is long. In California it can be felt in other Mudéjar windows and doors in the churches at Santa Barbara, Ventura (San Buenaventura), San Fernando, and San Luis Rey. No doubt an expert could discern it more ubiquitously than that. If this influence were acknowledged, the most complete, and probably the most widely read, book on the California missions would be less likely to refer to the "striking star window" at Carmel as "a frequent source of speculation, some viewers concluding that it should be placed on its side as a rectangle rather than balanced on one point as a star."

Above: A window at Carmel.

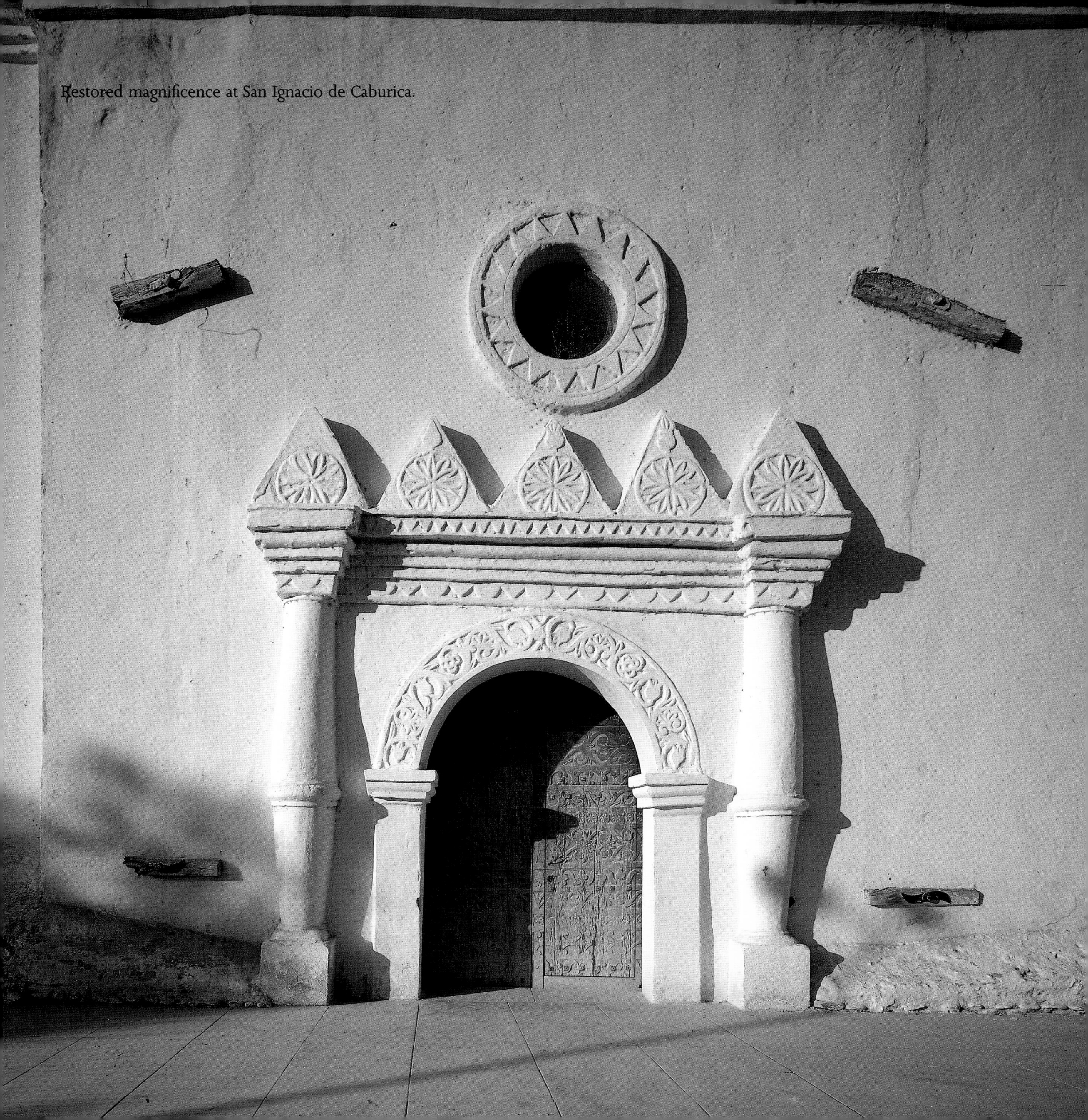

Restored magnificence at San Ignacio de Caburica.

It is devoutly to be wished that someone who has a wide acquaintance with Islamic architecture would give us a thorough account of how that tradition is expressed in the New World missions, especially the hundreds created in the sixteenth century when the example of Moorish Spain was still fresh in the minds of the builders. There are many diamond-shaped windows, doors tucked in at the midriff, and horseshoe arches.

Nothing is simple, though. We often take the horseshoe arch to be Moorish. In a sense it is, because it joined the currency of architecture in Spain and in Spanish colonies because of its frequent use by the Mudéjar, some of whom were, broadly speaking, Moorish. But as I noted early on, the horseshoe arch was used by the Visigoths, who passed it along to the Moors. Two horseshoe arches separated by a little column became one template for Moorish windows, taken up with enthusiasm by the Mission Style of the 1920s. Crossed horseshoes became spearheads, and crossed spearheads became stalactite ceilings in the Alhambra and in the little chapels of Mexico, where one can find the full complexity of the Iberian, Visigothic, North African, Mozarabic, Mudéjar, Mexican, Indian tradition.

A quatrefoil window from Magdalena, Sonora.

Below: The scalloped doorway, emblematic of respect for the creatures of the sea, is both an Old World and a New World motif. This is a doorway from the church of San Antonio del Oquitoa, Sonora, Mexico.

THE COMING OF THE RENAISSANCE

The Renaissance and the Middle Ages arrived in America together. The first palaces in the New World were products of the ambition of the Columbuses, father and son, Cristóbal and Diego (Christopher and John), who as much as Gutenberg and Galileo exemplified the questioning spirit of the rebirth of classical learning and Roman architecture.

Though the Columbian churches were Gothic, Diego's palace, built soon after 1510 and still to be seen in Santo Domingo, was in a Renaissance style so novel that only one or two buildings like it existed at the time in Spain itself. Diego's city was planned with equal daring. His grid plan around a plaza was much like that of Santa Fe, the military encampment outside the walls of Granada at which his father had received the blessing of Ferdinand and Isabella for his voyage. That plan reappeared all through Latin America and as far north as Santa Fe, New Mexico, but it appeared on Hispaniola while such rectilinearity was new and rare in Spain.

Diego's palace of 1509 had arcaded loggias like those employed by Palladio fifty years later in Italy: one atop the other, inset on both of its long facades, producing an elongated H-plan with a great assembly room in the center. When Hernán Cortés felt sufficiently confident of his conquest of Mexico in 1519, he adopted Diego's proclamative style and built a similar palace, which still exists, in Cuernavaca. The style is "proclamative" because neither palace is defensible; both assert that the neighborhood has been "pacified."

(Stratford Hall, the birthplace of Robert E. Lee, in Virginia, built on the Virginia frontier two hundred years later, is the only American manor house to use this symmetrical H-plan. It is, however, much smaller and plainer than the palaces of Columbus and Cortés.)

The Church ruled the Middle Ages and trained its missionaries in convents (places where either men or women or both come together — convenire — for religious purposes) built according to medieval practices. From such gathering places missionaries later dispersed, but graven upon their memories was the pattern of what a proper church should be. They carried the recollections of old convents just as crabs carry a shell-building pattern for formation when the old carapace is shed. The friars reconstructed, from Hispaniola to Manila, the essential qualities of the medieval places where they had learned their vocation. Thus was the medieval tradition sustained nearly into the nineteenth century in remote provinces such as California and Texas. Gothicisms and traces of the Romanesque still appeared there, because the church was very conservative indeed.

The captains of Spain, however, had no such memories. They felt no need to use familiar architecture to contain familiar doctrine. The conquistadors were on the make, and they made immediate use of the very latest fashions. Accordingly, the palaces they built in the Americas were from the outset in the Renaissance style, with only a few provincial lapses in detail.

By 1525 both the medievalism of the Church and the high-style Renaissance of the captains could be observed on Hispaniola. Expeditions from that island had been successful in Mexico, Yucatán, and Central America, and the two styles of building were juxtaposed in those places as well.

There is a continuing dialogue between the medievalism of the architects of this first period of Catholic building in the Americas and the advanced taste of the conquistadors. The architects for most of their buildings are unknown, but from the names we can identify we can determine that many of the secular builders were Spanish or Indian military engineers, and many of those who presided over the construction of churches were Flemings, like the Franciscan Peter of Ghent. Some Spanish architects and craftsmen contracted for work in America as early as 1510.

Their achievement, and that of their Indian work force, is as astonishing as the pyramids of Egypt or the Great Wall of China, and considerably more interesting in its diversity.

PLANS

Floor plans, or, as architects call them, "footprints," are clues more potent than facades to original purpose. What is the nature of a building? How was it intended to be used by those who built it? We must be careful not to trust its persona, its facade, because ever since the theatrical Greeks began the European tradition of building for effect, looks have deceived. This is as true of the architecture of Dodge City or Deadwood as of the magic of Barnum and David Copperfield. We are properly wary of the apparently obvious. There is often more truth to be found in shadow, the ecology in which floor plans grow. Shadow is the habitat of dreams, of the unconscious, and, less glamorously, of habit.

Shared habit extended in time becomes tradition, and tradition is often expressed in floor plans. The footprints of the Renaissance palaces anxiously established upon New World earth by the conquistadors lead back by a fairly straightforward route to the form makers of Rome and Florence. The floor plans of the mission churches built at the time are more eloquent, but they require a little explanation.

The plans fall into a number of obvious categories. Some are similar to each other because they were built to the same designs, distributed by a central authority. In the Russian colonial tradition, including their mission churches in California and Alaska, as in Siberia, that authority was political. The Spanish government did not issue detailed standard programs to be followed in building missions, nor did the religious orders, even the Jesuits, require uniformity. (None of the mission churches still existing in what is now the United States were constructed under the supervision of Jesuits. In Arizona the sites were selected by them, but all the present churches were constructed by Indians directed by Franciscans.) As a result, there is no distinction to be made between Franciscan and Jesuit ornament or floor plans.

Jesuit authority came with the scholarly Erasmians of the Counter Reformation, a classically sophisticated ecclesiastical elite that came to Mexico shortly after Cortés. For a long time the Franciscans, Augustinians, and Dominicans were more conservative, architecturally, than the Jesuits, but by the end of the eighteenth century they were in general agreement. The expulsion of the Jesuits in 1767 did not alter the generally Jesuitical nature of the most ambitious of mission churches built thereafter, such as San Xavier del Bac.

After 1600 the Erasmians, perhaps more powerful in Mexico than in Spain itself, made their classicizing influence tangible by distributing architectural manuals grounded in the lessons of the ancients — or, rather, in Italian impressions of the ancients. It is often said that Spanish-language versions of the works of the Roman architect Vitruvius were available in California, Mexico, and Texas. That is true, but it gives too little credit to Italian and Spanish ingenuity, for the renderings of Vitruvius did not survive the Middle Ages. Only his descriptions of early Roman and Hellenistic buildings were accessible to Renaissance architects who attached to his text their own drawings. One such rendering was used for the mission at Santa Barbara in California and for the facade of the Royal Chapel (La Capella Real), designed by Manuel Ruiz and completed in the same year, 1794, as his more famous and considerably less Vitruvian mission church of San Carlos Borromeo at Carmel.

There is great controversy among scholars as to how much of the architecture of the missions represents patterns carried from the Old World and how much springs from the genius of the Americans who did the actual work. There is little to be gained by attempts to allocate each scroll, motif, and gradation of color to either Europe or America. There is no dispute among those who have studied the matter in recent years that Indians, mulattos, and mestizos, people of many genetic inheritances, contributed not just the hard labor of construction but also the actual design and supervision of entire buildings as well as sculptured and painted ornament. It would not be right to fail to note the artists and architects whose names are known to us, so a short list is given in the Appendix.

HALL CHURCHES IN THE FRANCISCAN STYLE

MEXICO: There are scores of these. The most famous, having full panoply of Gothic vaulting and long, thin, single-aisled shape, are at Tapeaca and Huejotzingo in Puebla.

NEW MEXICO: San Esteban del Rey de Acoma, San Isidro.

CALIFORNIA: San Antonio de Padua, San Gabriel Arcángel, San Diego de Alcalá, San Francisco de Asis, San Antonio de Pala, Santa Inés.

1 Nave
2 Apse, sanctuary
3 Sacristy

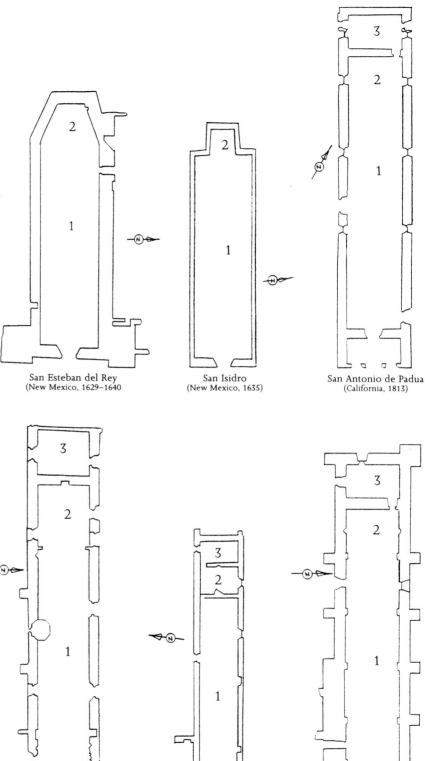

San Esteban del Rey
(New Mexico, 1629–1640)

San Isidro
(New Mexico, 1635)

San Antonio de Padua
(California, 1813)

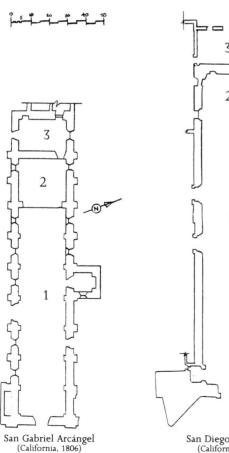

San Gabriel Arcángel
(California, 1806)

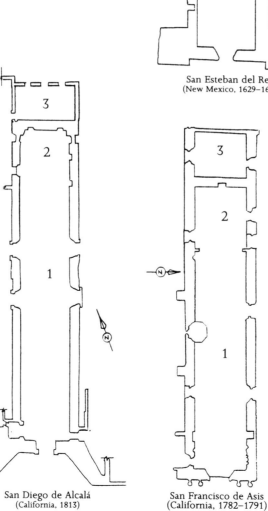

San Diego de Alcalá
(California, 1813)

San Francisco de Asis
(California, 1782–1791)

San Antonio de Pala
(California, 1813)

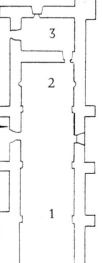

Santa Inés
(California, 1817)

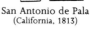

81

CRUCIFORM

TEXAS: San Francisco de la Espada: but not as reconstructed. Nuestra Señora de la Purísima Concepción: similar in plan to San Xavier del Bac*. San Antonio de Valero*: virtually identical to la Purísima Concepción in plan, but bigger by a fifth.

ARIZONA: San Xavier del Bac*. San José de Tumacácori was intended to be its duplicate.

NEW MEXICO: Nuestra Señora de los Angeles (Pecos): the 1705 church. Ranchos de Taos: sacristy extends one arm of transept. Trampas: the new church. San Buenaventura (Gran Quivira): small projections did house side altars, but inconspicuously; baptistry and sacristy not truly cruciform. Nuestra Señora de la Purísima Concepción de Quarai: front crossing added later.

CALIFORNIA: San Luis Rey de Francia: but with a hexagonal side chapel. San Juan Capistrano: but with a sacristy between the sanctuary and one arm of the transept.

*These have a second set of projections, appearing in plan like a second crossing, but housing baptistries or sacristies near the entrance. The church at Acoma has a pair of bell towers in front plus a sacristy accessible through the cloister, so it also has an "L," or perhaps its own format.

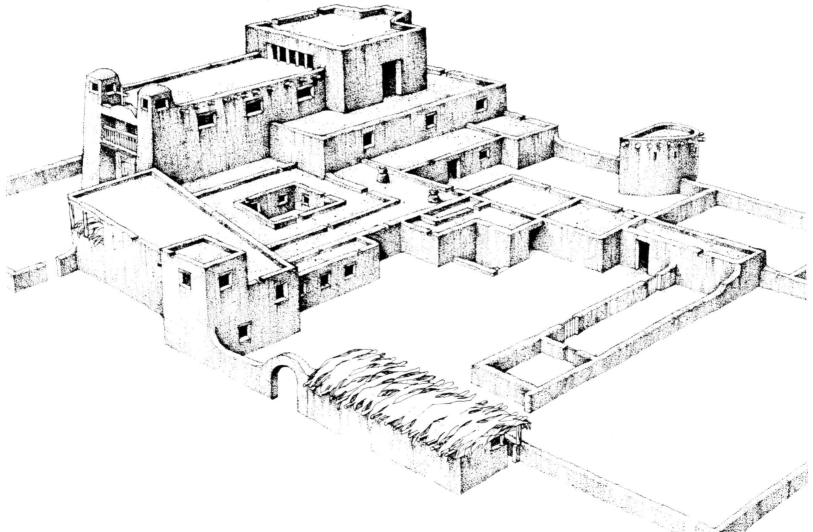

THE SECOND PECOS CHURCH

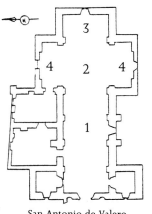

San Antonio de Valero
(The Alamo, Texas, 1755)

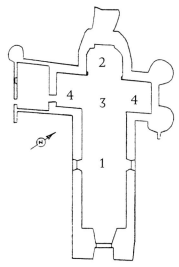

Ranchos de Taos Church
(New Mexico, 1772)

Pecos
(New Mexico, 1717)

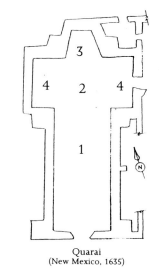

Quarai
(New Mexico, 1635)

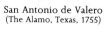

1 Nave
2 Apse, sanctuary
3 Sacristy
4 Vestry

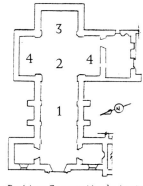

La Purísima Concepción de Acuña
(Texas, 1731)

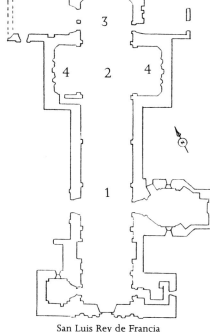

San Luis Rey de Francia
(California, 1815)

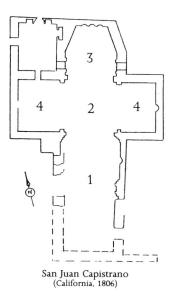

San Juan Capistrano
(California, 1806)

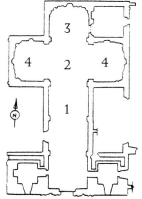

San Xavier del Bac
(Arizona, 1797)

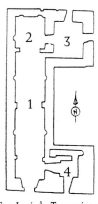

San José de Tumacácori
(Arizona, 1822)

HALL CHURCHES WITH A SACRISTY, BAPTISTRY, OR OTHER "L" PROJECTION

TEXAS (San Antonio): San Juan Capistrano: hexagonal sacristy at east end, baptistry at base of bell tower at west end. San José y San Miguel de Aguayo: side chapel and baptistry in front, sacristy by the sanctuary, originally designed to be cruciform but transepts removed during construction.

NEW MEXICO: Nuestra Señora de los Angeles (Pecos): the 1680 church has tiny projections that are more or less cruciform but contain side chapel and baptistry, not two side chapels. Nuestra Señora de Guadalupe de Zuñi. San José de Laguna: sacristy and baptistry. San José de Guisewa (Jémez): probably the only frontier church with true clerestory windows, rather than windows in a raised projection, like a choir loft set transversely. San Gregorio de Abó: sacristy and baptistry similar to those at Gran Quivira, with the plan flipped over; James Ivey says it is the closest American church to those Mexican churches called by George Kubler "cryptocollateral." Side chapels two feet deep, made almost secret by screens that retain the line of the walls of the nave.

CALIFORNIA: San Luis Obispo: chapel — original? Santa Bárbara: choir and baptistry. San Miguel Arcángel: sacristy. San Buenaventura.

ARIZONA: San José de Tumacácori: baptistry and sacristy in final plan. Designed to be transepted or cruciform with a sacristy like a foot to the cross.

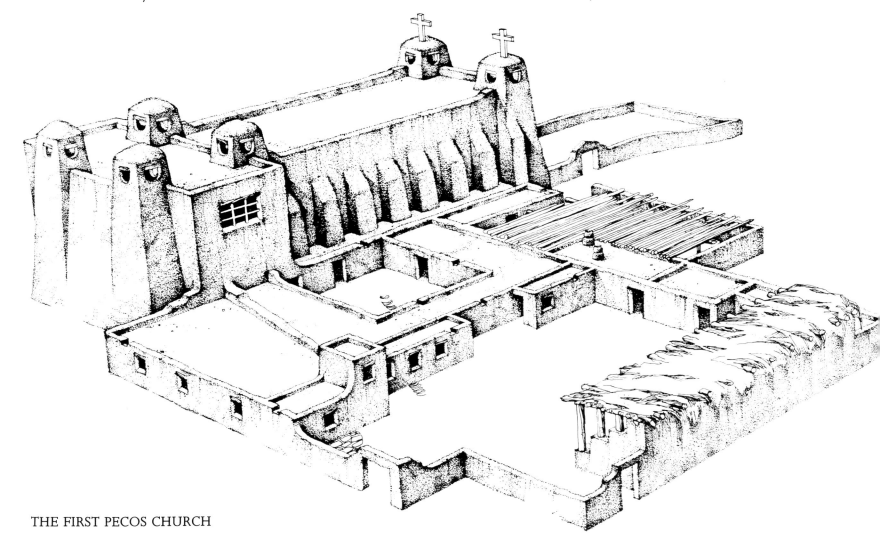

THE FIRST PECOS CHURCH

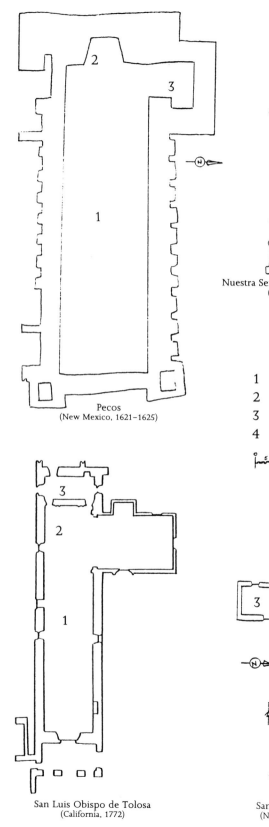

Pecos
(New Mexico, 1621–1625)

Nuestra Señora de Guadalupe de Zuñi
(New Mexico, 1699)

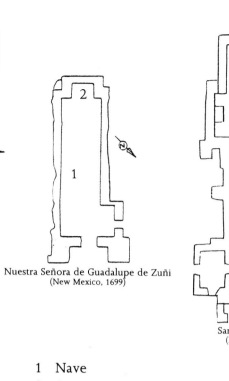

San Gregorio de Abó
(New Mexico, 1670)

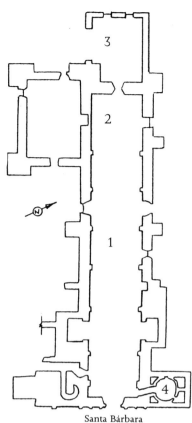

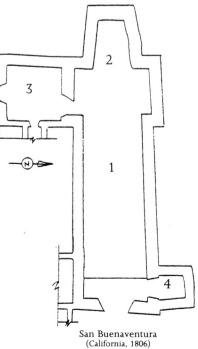

Santa Bárbara
(California, 1820)

1 Nave
2 Apse, sanctuary
3 Sacristy
4 Vestry

San Luis Obispo de Tolosa
(California, 1772)

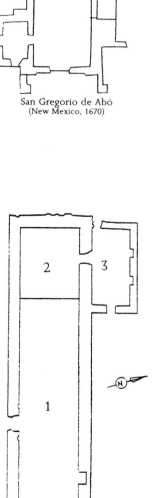

San José de Laguna
(New Mexico, 1706)

San Miguel Arcángel
(California, 1818)

San Buenaventura
(California, 1806)

85

A BRIEF HISTORY OF THE DOME

The creation of domes is a proclamation of human pride. It asserts that humankind may participate in the ordering of the universe. The fame of heroes echoes from the dome of heaven. They may appropriately be interred within a form that makes the point for those who missed it the first time. The earliest Christian saints and martyrs were put to rest in round, domed buildings, called martyria, traditional forms borrowed from ancient heroes' tombs and from the sanctuaries of mystery cults. Tucson is not too distant, architecturally, from Jerusalem; the dome of the Church of the Holy Sepulchre is one prototype for the dome of San Xavier del Bac. The dome is also Christianity's supreme expression of deference to the ancient mystery cults of the Middle East, which provided the form of round, domed *mysteria*.

Alexander the Great conquered Asia as far as India using a domed tent as his headquarters, with symbols of the stars on the inner vault. The audience tents of his competitors, the Achaemenid kings of Persia and the rulers of upper India, were dome-shaped as well. Alexander's successors, the Ptolemaic kings of Egypt, ruled in rooms made to look like tents, with the corners of their domes crinkled as if made of canvas. It was the memory of Alexander that filled the imagination of the twenty-six-year-old emperor Nero when he built his Golden House in Rome. Beneath its revolving cupola of wood painted with the stars, he received his guests as a second Alexander and as *kosmokrator*. Nero and his architects, like Trajan and those he later summoned to design his Pantheon, were well aware of the evocative power of round, domed buildings.

Later Christian emperors such as Justinian and Charlemagne also invoked that tradition when they built their own mausoleums and imperial chapels. Domes are not easy to build. Northern Europe could not summon the energy or skill for them after the eclipse of Rome in the fifth century until the sixteenth, except during the glorious, brief Frankish decades that came to an end with the death of Charlemagne in 814.

Charlemagne's contribution to Arizona was not inconsiderable. His mausoleum at Aachen provided another link in the chain of the mysteria and martyria, the Golden House of Nero, the Pantheon of Hadrian, and the baroque aspirations of the friars. For the Roman and Holy Roman emperors, the dome was a grand baldachin, emphasizing that they were demigods, or wished to be thought so. Their provision of huge, solid halos for themselves gathered potency from the older tradition of mysteria and martyria, which can still be seen from the Caspian Sea to Gibraltar.

Holiness was a commodity of much value to Nero, Hadrian, and Charlemagne. Holiness was inherent in the form of an inverted bowl of sanctity, a constructed simulacrum of the heavens. In the heavens resided the gods, from whom all these imperial males received reassuring signs of favor. Under such inverted bowls many a later monarch appeared as king-as-saint, or at least king-as-friendly-to-the-church.

The Arabs of the desert, whose architecture had to be portable, carried their holy objects in tents with red leather domes. Similarly, their enemies, the Christians, were accustomed to carrying portable altars installed, like their bishops or emperors, under the little domical canopies we call baldachins. The most famous of these can be seen today in Saint Peter's, in Rome, though there are innumerable examples in Mexico and Arizona. The Arabs found the palaces they wrested from Alexander's successors compatibly arranged.

During the Middle Ages the Muslims used domes as the Romans had used them, to enclose large spaces such as baths and markets, but they did not emphasize them as the Byzantines did. The Muslim contribution to the dome building of American missions is not, therefore, to be seen in vast structures like San Xavier, but instead in little domes set in rows, like egg cartons turned upside down. The architect of the Mosque of an-Naqah in Tripoli made such a deployment. So, at several Spanish removes, did the designer of the open chapel of the Franciscan monastery in Cholula, Puebla. This very ancient form did not work its way into the mission buildings of the United States, but it is a good reminder that not all domes are set at crossings, and not all domes are imperial.

Opposite: Bells, domes, and white cement, a Mediterranean building material used masterfully by the Romans: the roof of San Ignacio de Caburica, Sonora.

San José de Tumacácori, Arizona,

American domes owe something to Islam, but more to the Council of Trent. The Council summoned Catholic Europe into simultaneous crusades against corruption and Protestantism at a crucial moment. Spain was collecting itself to sustain the assaults of Columbus, Cortés, and Coronado and readying itself to colonize what it had conquered, reaching out of the valley of Mexico toward the north and the south.

In 1563 the Council called for a Counter Reformation. The dome became one index of this movement, even in Mexico, where there was no Reformation to counter. In the hands of the Jesuits the dome was a symbol of the resurgence of the Church Militant, blazoning its confidence in mission churches in places as remote as Santo Angel de la Guarda de Satevo.

This astonishing, almost unknown building has survived at the bottom of the Barranca de Sinforosa, a remote and very deep canyon four miles from the expiring silver-mining center of Botopilas, in the area inhabited by the Tarahumara. (There is another, and considerably more accessible, Satevo fifty miles due south of Chihuahua. It, too, has a church, apparently contemporary to that near Botopilas, but modest in comparison.)

Though the mission church at Santo Angel is sometimes called the "lost cathedral," it is not a cathedral, because a cathedral is the seat of a bishop. But it is grand. It has three domes, one at the crossing, one atop the bell tower, and a third at midpoint on the nave, together with four half-domes and a vaulted ceiling. This is roughly the pattern of San Juan Capistrano; perhaps, if the Satevo church survives the pig farmers and lumber trucks that surround it and a likely rush of treasure hunters now that a hard-surfaced road into the canyon has been completed, it can instruct us how San Juan *would* have looked had the earthquakes and restorers been more gentle.

Even the domes at Satevo are not signs of a simple holiness. They bespeak an imperial religion — if not of an emperor, then of a pope, and if not of a pope, then of his soldier-servants, the militant members of the Society of Jesus. Imperially domes appeared in the metropolis of domes, Mexico City, in San Antonio, and at San Xavier del Bac. Imperially they were attempted in southern California and Texas. Imperially they glower out of the bottom of the Barranca de Sinforosa.

The Mission Santo Angel de la Guarda de Satevo, at the bottom of the Barranca del Cobre, Chihuahua.

When we come upon domes ornamented with little stars and planets in mission churches, we can remember how Alexander, having called himself the Son of Heaven, and Nero, *kosmokrator*, bestowed upon the world the cosmic dome, and how the king of Parthia sat in a judgment hall "the ceiling of which was constructed in the form of a dome like the heavens, covered with sapphire stone, this stone being intensely blue and of the color of the sky . . . and in its heights are the images of the gods in whom they believed, and they appear golden."

Amid the rubble of San Juan Capistrano in California are the fragments of seven domes. The most ambitious of all American missions, San Juan, actually did achieve its intentions for a brief time. But California is a high-risk environment for dome makers; the San Andreas Fault readjusted the mission's stance a few years after completion, and the Baroque lost its western citadel.

Domes are symbols of several things, among them royalty. Of the few surviving missions with a dome, two commemorate a king or queen. One is San Luis Rey de Francia in California, dedicated to the crusading king of France. The second, La Purísima Concepción, in Texas, is dedicated to the queen of heaven.

A memory of Middle Eastern heroes' tombs: Jesuit domes at Satevo.

In Texas San José y San Miguel and in Arizona San José de Tumacácori have domes. San Antonio de Valero (the Alamo) was striving for one; the arches and supports were completed, but by 1793 the resident population of Indians had declined to a handful of families. Disease and defection had done their work: no magic had come from the hands of friars. "Secularization" of the missions in Texas, as in California somewhat later, was not a sudden, brutish, political obliteration of a thriving enterprise. It was a recognition of the failure of a grand but flawed venture.

The Franciscans abandoned their mission attempt at the Alamo. They had possibly saved some souls and had ministered to many bodies, though the microbes brought by Europeans had infected many. Architecturally, they had achieved enough by placing domes at the crossings of the two other churches in San Antonio, a sufficient recompense for what they had learned from the Jesuits and a sufficient statement of the architectural doctrines of the Counter Reformation.

By 1801 the shell of the Alamo was untended; the sacristy was in use as a military chapel. A small army of Louisiana freebooters, the first set of soldiers of fortune to use the Alamo as a fortress, arrived in 1813. Antonio López de Santa Anna then made his first successful assault upon this venerable hulk, driving out the free-booters and dealing with the survivors in his customary expeditious way.

The church was partly fortified again in 1835; the Anglos were attempting to complete that work when Santa Anna appeared in February 1836 as dictator of Mexico. The bullet-pocked sanctuary was put to service as the final redoubt into which limped Davy Crockett, Jim Bowie, and the rash coeur-de-lion William Barret Travis, commander of the outmanned and outgeneraled advance guard of the Republic of Texas. When Santa Anna hauled up the red flag of "no quarter" on the tower of the nearby parish church (today transmogrified into the Cathedral of Saint Anthony), he presided over the first step in the creation of a new set of heroes. He completed that process by his slaughter of the handful of survivors who had defended the Alamo to the last cartridge and then surrendered.

The San Antonio missions remain, full of ghosts and memories, strange in their urban setting. The steel-and-glass bank headquarters on the skyline vaunt themselves at the expense of the modest accomplishments of the friars. The bankers themselves are not doing much vaunting; admonitions toward humility and even, in some cases, toward poverty have been provided by the comptroller of the currency. But the skyscrapers of the vainglorious 1980s are still there.

San Carlos Borromeo de Carmelo.

92

Beyond the power of Europe lies the countryside, eternal, with its own imperatives: looking across the roof of San Ignacio de Caburica. This site was chosen by Father Kino in 1687; the present church was built after 1753.

THOUGHTS AT SAN XAVIER DEL BAC

Now that California's San Juan Capistrano has been reduced to rubble and romance, there is no better place to find evidence of the majesty of the American missions without cropping the picture than to go at sunset to the shimmering white half-spheres of San Xavier del Bac in Arizona. One comes to San Xavier around brown corners of rock, out of the sweltering plain. It reposes in its own oasis, uncompromised by urban encroachment, unchallenged even by large trees, summoning a full panoply of devices to persuade the awed and acquiescent of the power of the Church Militant.

The domes of the church are said to be white, but nothing in the desert is truly white; they are pink or blue or orange or even green at different times of day. At dawn or sunset the sun caresses each dome in sequence, sun-symbol answering sun, dome of earth responding to dome of heaven, as each returns round greetings to the larger encompassing roundness.

The principal dome of San Xavier is set, as it should be in the Baroque canon, at the crossing of the transept, where the nave approaches the altar, having received the assurance of the militant towers set about the portal. This is a frontier church; these towers are neither identical nor symmetrical, because one was never finished to plan. (The same fate befell the symmetrical aspirations of San José y San Miguel in Texas.) When one sees unequal towers, a minaret lurks in the background. This is not a North European church with two equal towers topping a battlemented "westwork" (the fortified west end of an early Romanesque church).

Mexico became a country of domes (as Syria once was) but not until the first missionary zeal of the mendicant orders had passed. These domes were built after 1650 or so, well after most of the Franciscan, Dominican, and Augustinian building in central Mexico was completed.

San Xavier del Bac, Arizona.

94

San Xavier is a collection point of history, reaching back into the imperial past of the Mediterranean. It is no wonder that it seems, against its green hillside in the spring and against the brown grass of the late fall, so like a vision of Syria or Sicily or Morocco. There are churches like it in Mexico, and others in Spain. No other mission church, except perhaps that at Satevo, can so irresistibly guide us back toward the origins of the imperial spirit that flowed from the cockpit of Mediterranean energy into America.

The dome at San Xavier rests upon an octagonal drum, which, like its towers, recalls Islamic forms as well as American sacred structures four centuries older than those of the Arabs.

Though the California missions are often very grand indeed — Santa Bárbara comes instantly to mind — the Franciscans there, unlike their brothers around San Antonio, Texas, and in Arizona, did not much favor the Jesuit penchant for imperial domes. This was true even though they had amply demonstrated that they could instruct an Indian work force in making round vaults — a task beyond the skills of the English colonists until after 1795.

With the few exceptions we have noted and a handful more in Mexico itself, the domes of the Spanish missions are monuments either of truimphant Jesuitism or of those late Franciscans and Dominicans who assumed the role of soldiers of the papacy after the Jesuits were expelled in 1767.

The Jesuit-Franciscan transition is important enough to those contemplating a tour of the churches of Padre Kino in Arizona and northern Mexico to justify a paragraph of emphasis from the Jesuit scholar Charles W. Polzer:

> None of the imposing Spanish colonial churches still standing today, however, were the handiwork of Padre Kino himself. The splendid buildings at San Xavier del Bac, Caborca and Tubutama represent the last flourish of Franciscan efforts in a land they inherited from the expelled Jesuits. All of these churches were erected nearly a century after Kino had established the first missions in these widespread pueblos.

> Less than a quarter century after Kino's death most of the proud structures he had personally built with his team of skilled craftsmen were crumbling into

ruin. . . . All that remains of the personal work of Padre Kino are a few deeply protected adobes inside the walls of Cocóspera and under the mounded ruins of Delores and Remedios. . . . Now they are only sad monuments to the ravages of weather, Indian wars, revolutions, and blindly ignorant treasure hunters.

Father Polzer's reference to Caborca and to Tubutama, both in Mexico, remind us to urge readers to visit these magnificent survivors, so similar to San Xavier and so little appreciated.

La Purísima Concepción de Nuestra Señora de Caborca lies in a fertile valley worthy of the affection of Padre Kino, who founded a Jesuit mission here in 1693. The present church, dedicated by the Franciscans, was completed in 1809. Its design, probably by Ignacio Gaona, follows that of San Xavier del Bac. (Gaona probably had a hand in the design of San Xavier, which was completed before 1797; the two are quite similar.)

The mission at Caborca has always been endangered; the Pima drove out the Jesuits in 1695 and drove them out again in their great revolt in 1751. In 1857 Henry A. Crabb and his filibusters attempted to capture the sanctuary, which was used by the local population as a fortress; Crabb's men were defeated and executed on the front steps. After floods destroyed the back end of La Purísima Concepción, it was rebuilt as a national monument. It is only rarely used for liturgical purposes.

San Pedro y San Pablo del Tubutama was established under Padre Kino's direction in 1687. During the Pima Rebellion of 1751, the Jesuit church built by Padre Jacobo Sedelmayr around 1750 was burned. The rebuilt church was reduced to ruins by 1780 and rebuilt on its present, grander lines by the Franciscans under Father Barbatro in 1788. Though American treasure hunters dynamited the pueblo in the 1950s, the church survived. The facade, with mannerist Baroque ornamentation set about a Moorish doorway, and a minaret bell tower, shows how Tumacácori might have appeared had it been completed.

La Purísima Concepción de Nuestra Señora de Caborca in Sonora. The mission was founded by Father Kino in 1693; the present church was built between 1803 and 1809.

BELLS AND WHISTLES

The sound of a policeman's whistle — a familiar sign of authority — means "stop." The mission bells meant both "stop" and "start." They prescribed the alteration of the Indians' day from one regulated by individual inclination, or by the sun, moon, and stars, to one prescribed by the military or by the economic requirements of the mission. The commands of mission bells were so imperative that bells became objects of loathing to many mission Indians; they were brought down from their towers during the Pueblo Revolt of 1670 and ceremonially smashed. Bells signaled the start of a day of forced labor and reminded the exhausted construction workers and field hands that even as the cold seeped out of the widening desert shadows, the friars and soldiers were still regulating their lives. And would be there again in the morning.

> The Mission bell told me
> That we'd never part . . .

Mission bells have found their way into the soundtrack of romance, just as the openwork *espadaña*, the perforated wall housing the bells, has joined its scenery. The reality was not so sweet. Nonetheless the mission bell, even when electronically simulated (as it often is these days), seems to us a pleasant sound. The Franciscans put a great emphasis upon good bells. They established a *maestro campanero*, Hernán Sanchez, in Mexico City as early as 1612; his handiwork can still be heard there. The bell at Acoma, New Mexico, like those smashed at Pecos and Awatovi, was molded about 1710.

It is the *espadañas* of Texas and California that attract sketchbooks and wonder, rather than the bell towers or even the bell-stressing heightened facades of San Francisco de la Espada in Texas, San José de Laguna in New Mexico, or San Luis Obispo in California. In the facades of Laguna and Santo Domingo and in the courtyard gate at Ranchos de Taos, the bells are joined with a cloud motif that meant power of a different but equally potent sort to the Indians themselves.

Bells: human discipline replaces the rhythms of the sun and moon.

The Texas San Juan Capistrano and its California brother (because the bell tower is gone and the bells have been given a new housing in a wall) and many of the other California missions center upon these freestanding icon holders. The iconography is of power — power over time.

Something subtle and very moving has occurred in some of these places. At Pala the parishioners insisted that the *campanario* be rebuilt after a flood washed it away. The sound of the bells was no longer a signal to work, but rather a signal to worship, as we prefer to think that it has always been.

What is the history of this auditory icon? Bells were not part of Roman or Egyptian culture. Cymbals or rattles made their summoning percussions. Indeed, bells do not appear to have been employed in the Eastern rites until the eighth or ninth century. Stationary bells, composed of four flat sides of metal struck by a moving clapper, were made in France, Ireland, and England around 550. The Venerable Bede was proud of his bells, and the Irish monks took a four-sided bell with them to Saint Gall, Switzerland, by 646. A *campana* was a large bell used in a tower, or *campanile*.

Bells as symbols of authority were fought over in the Middle Ages, for they generally summoned soldiers to battle. To this day, town councils in obstreperous cities such as Antwerp own the bell that tolls curfew (*couvre-feu*, or "cover the fires," meaning, essentially, blackout time). The principal bell in many cathedrals is owned by the town, not by the chapter. Bells tolled the commencement of religious massacre on St. Bartholomew's Eve in 1571, when 100,000 French Protestants died, and of a national rising on the third day of Easter in 1282 — the Sicilian vespers. The death knell of 8,000 Frenchmen was set to music, notably without many bells, by Verdi.

William the Conqueror invented the eight o'clock curfew, and other Normans brought a bell-tolling society to the Mediterranean. It is odd but true that while the *campanile* is ubiquitous in Catholic countries, the wall pierced with apertures displaying bells seems to have flourished only in Spain, Mexico, and the American Southwest. Perhaps a southern light goes best through a wall rendered almost invisible at dawn and dusk, as the bells seem to hover, held in place by the light itself.

The bells of San Miguel Arcángel call the attentive traveler to
the California mission church that remains closest to its original
condition.

San José at Laguna Pueblo here the Spanish parapet merged
with the Pueblo cloud motif.

A NOTE ON BLOOD AND COLUMNS

Some mention must be made of the related phenomena of bloody loincloths and extraneous columns and pilasters in the missions. (Ramon Gutierrez has written what must surely be the definitive discussion of these subjects.) Peculiar freestanding pilasters and columns are found in many, if not most, of the California missions, and in the painted ornament of several in New Mexico. In many others, the original painted plasterwork, which may have borne depictions of columns, lies in fragments or has been lost to whitewash. These columns support nothing and do not imply that they were to be seen as part of any structural scheme. They are objects presented singly.

The Franciscans had a tradition of flagellation at posts, columns, or trees. Sometimes mortification of the flesh was administered by others with whips. Sometimes it was self-flagellation or self-injury with thorns or knives. For the Franciscans, flagellation was mortification of the flesh, a means of escaping imprisonment within that flesh.

The Pueblo Indians had a tradition grounded in an entirely different religious sense, which happened to entail flagellation as well. Pueblo war chiefs were whipped with cacti to demonstrate their resistance to pain; in the Hopi, Zuñi, and Tewa pueblos, Cactus War Societies initiated their members and manifested membership in this way. In the Hopi Snake Dance observed by Hernán Gallegos in 1582, "The participants flagellated themselves with cactus pods and then whipped the 'lord' until they drew blood, making him look like a flagellant." Gutierrez says that "from the Pueblos south to the Maya, bloodletting was tied to rulership and the mythology of the cosmic order. . . . At every important religious event, men shed blood by flagellating themselves, by lacerating . . . cutting incisions into various parts of the body, thus feeding the gods and expressing piety. Blood shed from the penis was particularly nourishing because it would bring rain."

Before these two traditions — Catholic and Indian — merged in Mexico, there was no Christian tradition of bloody loincloths in crucifixion scenes. And in no group of buildings except those in the American Southwest and in Mexico does a single column with no structural function, sometimes flecked with red, appear prominently and frequently in painted ornament and upon walls. This motif seems always to be associated with the Franciscans, not with the Jesuits, Dominicans, or Augustinians, who did not have a tradition of bloody mortification. And, like the cloud motifs associated with saintly figures in sculpture, the column seems to represent a merging of two cultures at the point at which the physical becomes the metaphysical.

The altar and railing of Nuestra Señora de la Asunción at Zia Pueblo, New Mexico.

Opposite: Columns, three-dimensional and painted on the wall, at San José de Guadalupe in Fremont, California.

The red-painted columns along the nave of San Antonio de
Pala, California.

PART IV
ALONG THE MISSION FRONTIER

FLORIDA AND THE ISLANDS

THERE IS MUCH TRUTH IN THE CLICHÉ that the Spaniards came to America for God, gold, and glory; clichés are the oatmeal of discourse, never exciting but often nutritious. But we can do without this formula if it persuades anyone that the other colonizers — Swedes, Dutch, French, and British — came to these shores indifferent to these factors, or that these were the *only* motivations of the men and women who sailed to America from Spanish ports.

Even the English had God in mind. Their God was not as interested in Indians as the Spanish and French God was, but even the English tried conversion. Twenty-five communities of "praying Indians" sprang up on Martha's Vineyard, on Nantucket, and in the Plymouth Colony; there were four in territory claimed by Massachusetts Bay. Even the Virginia Company, not renowned for its philanthropic interests, received a series of royal urgings to undertake conversion; funds allocated for that purpose never seem to have found their way to Indians, however.

In the eighteenth century, Quakers and Moravians established missions on the Pennsylvania and Ohio frontiers, thereby inadvertently exposing their converts to massacre by other Christian frontiersmen. These were not the first Protestant martyrs to the faith among the Indians; the English had used their converts as scouts and skirmishers against the French, Abenaki, and Iroquois. Many died for their devotion. The French and Spaniards had Indian allies as well, as our term "French *and* Indian Wars" suggests.

As the dynastic wars of Europe spilled over into America, sectarian excuses were found for the most dreadful acts of European barbarism in Texas and Florida, as in the Netherlands and central Germany.

It is important to know whose God we are invoking when we speak of service to God. It is likewise important to set aside any formula that tries to limit Spanish motivations to God, gold, and glory. That would deny us the full story of the Spanish missions of Florida.

The Spaniards did come seeking gold, but they did not long bemuse themselves with it. Next they pressed on to seek slaves, and, in the final stage, the one most closely connected to the implantation of their missions, they engaged in purely mercantile colonization, of the sort we would expect of the English.

As we discussed earlier, medieval Spain, specifically medieval Catalonia and Aragon, established a commercial empire in the Mediterranean similar to those of Genoa and Florence. If a European or a Muslim thought of a "typical Spaniard," the mental image would more likely be of a merchant from Barcelona than of a *hidalgo* from Castile. Though the dawn of the sixteenth century was the twilight of Spain as a commercial and industrial power, the impulse for trade and for trading colonies was far from dead by the 1540s, when the de Soto expedition found Spanish merchandise in Tennessee. There was very little missionary activity in the first generation of Spanish penetration in the New World. Columbus and his son Diego were busy eradicating Indians who resisted them and forcing the more tractable into working surface mines for gold. They operated under royal charters to exploit the people and the land they found for economic advantage. The early churches in Florida, as at La Isabela and Puerto Real, were garrison churches, not centers of serious missionary activity.

The Spanish mission churches in Florida looked much like this conjectural reconstruction of a church in La Florida, based on archaeological excavations at San Juan de Aspalaga.

The conquests of Jamaica and Cuba were not missionary endeavors, nor were Ponce de León's two assaults upon Florida in 1513 and 1521. In 1526, Lucas Vásquez de Ayllón took along three Dominicans to serve the religious requirements of the five hundred settlers he brought to the coast of South Carolina, but he brought many more tradesmen than priests. Theirs were the goods found by de Soto in the interior sixteen years later.

We must resist the temptation to treat these early colonists as if they were Phoenicians in Spain or Britons in Hong Kong: trade was not their primary purpose. Most of them were colonists, the majority, it seems, from the high green pasturelands of Asturias. Their king had told them they would find on the South Carolina shore "your own land . . . to farm, with . . . its pastures, woods, meadows, waters and rivers." Waters and rivers they got, together with fever, probably typhoid. Their colony was a swamp.

Spain launched seven expeditions against the Indians of Florida. The leaders of the first four died in disgrace and failure. None attempted missionary activity on any discernible scale. Their effects upon the inhabitants were entirely pernicious; the diseases they brought completed the massacre (the word is too strong only as to intention, not as to effect) of six million or more Indians in the islands and the American Southeast.

Finally the survivors of failed expeditions and the survivors of the Great Dying were given together into the hands of the Church. In the history of Spanish Florida it is impossible to separate actions induced by a desire to bring souls to Christ from those arising from the chivalric lust for glory, a passionate fealty to king and nation, or from the avarice of traders and the longing for land. There was ample land in "Florida" as it was described in the sixteenth century: it extended from the Chesapeake to the Sabine River, and perhaps to the Rio Grande. Because that land was attractive to Protestant Englishmen and to Protestant Frenchmen, Catholic Spaniards in Florida could feel patriotism ("fealty" is probably a better term for their feeling at this stage of history) in perfect harmony with religious zeal.

Pedro Menéndez de Avilés was among the most prescient of those Spaniards, a statesman equal to Benjamin Franklin in span of vision and ambition, for himself and for his countrymen. Menéndez envisaged a Spanish suzerainty from Newfoundland to Texas and linked to the empire of Cortés. He was the founder of the Castilian Empire in southeastern North America, taking possession of a grant of twenty-five square leagues, large enough to gain him a marquisate.

Menéndez owed fealty to the king of Castile, but he was not a nobleman. He never annexed the title "Don" to his name; we are led to think of other violent dons when we hear him described as a contractual conqueror by anthropologists such as David Hurst Thomas. Like Franklin, Menéndez was a bourgeois, but unlike Franklin, he was too early to make that status a virtue. The bourgeoisie of Menéndez's time were the medieval merchant conquerors who set forth from Pisa, Venice, Genoa, and Barcelona. They subjugated the old kingdoms, substituted the rule of contract for the code of honor, put their poniards into the entrails of feudalism, and created the modern world.

God, glory, and gold? Any legal tender, even an enforceable promise to pay, would do.

More than anyone else, Menéndez gave greater Florida the Spanish configuration it retained for two hundred years. He landed his expeditionary force, a thousand strong, at St. Augustine in 1565. There were few priests among them. The French, representing the still powerful Protestant party at court, had intruded upon the Spanish field of exploitation; they built Fort Caroline at what is now Jacksonville in 1562, thereby threatening the course of Spanish remittance from the mines of Mexico. In a series of massacres, murders after surrender, mutilations, and tortures beyond anything the observant Indians had ever seen, the French and Spaniards extended to the Florida and South Carolina coasts the

religious and dynastic wars that had already brought ruin to northern Italy and many valleys of the Pyrenees. Not until 1580 did Menéndez manage to exterminate the last vestiges of French resistance. Along the way he was forced to resist as well the predations of other Protestant contenders, English pirates led by Sir Francis Drake.

Drake replenished his ships in Florida and, after rounding Tierra del Fuego, refitted in California. So far as we know, he never attempted to convert an Indian to the Protestant persuasion, though the Huguenots of South Carolina, with whom he was briefly in league against Menéndez, did so. The first Calvinist hymns sung in America, with lyrics in French, were heard under the palmettos of South Carolina in the 1560s.

Menéndez used Jesuits as his agents; a little later the French used them against Spain. By 1566 the French had penetrated deep into the interior of Florida; Menéndez rejoined by sending Juan Pardo and Father Sebastian Montero on a 500-mile journey inland to undo the work of the Protestants (charging that the Protestant devil and the Indian devil were the same). The first Jesuit outposts attempted were in south Florida; they failed. The natives already knew too much of Christians. Other attempts, this time in what is now South Carolina, also failed, but in 1572 the Ajacan mission was established even farther north, on the shore of Chesapeake Bay. It was near the place where the British would locate their Jamestown thirty-five years later. This Chesapeake mission lasted only five months; then the Indians killed all the priests.

Soon thereafter the Jesuits abandoned greater Florida completely. In 1573, soon before his death, Menéndez turned to the Franciscans. At first only one or two priests attempted some missionary activity; their work was made less credible because they were often preceded by slave traders or by soldiers bent upon pillage. The friars found many Indian towns in embers. But by 1597 a string of Franciscan missions extended from Cape Canaveral to St. Catherines Island in Georgia. In that year the Indians rose against religious and political imperialism, martyred five Franciscans, and sustained their resistance until driven into the interior in 1601.

Thirty years of intermittent warfare and intermittent attempts at recruitment of new Christians brought 1,200 Indians into the fold, killed many more, and produced a crop of martyred priests. Spain considered abandoning the effort, but its treasure fleet from Veracruz still had to pass Florida on its way to Cádiz, and Drake had made his point. Under the cypresses of that coast a hive of privateers might roost; better keep it patrolled. And, while patrolling, why not save some souls?

A new Franciscan bishop, Juan de las Cabeszas de Altamirano, sailed into the port of St. Augustine in March 1606. The population of the shoreline missions declined slowly over the next century from disease and disaffection. The bishop and his successors put their primary energies instead into a string of presidios and missions extending across northern Florida into what are now Georgia and Alabama. These became very productive grain-growing enterprises. They were also successful as small theocracies, much like the contemporary Jesuit establishments in Paraguay. The clergy, reigning like the Cluniacs of earlier days, established their own port city at St. Marks, on the Gulf Coast. This infuriated the merchants of St. Augustine and Menéndez's successor as governor, who believed himself still to have a personal and family monopoly on the benefits to be secured from the colony. In 1647 the Apalachee, incited by the merchants and the governor's coterie in the capital, rose against the Franciscans, martyred three of them, and burned seven of the missions. The Franciscans, who had their own direct capillaries to the Spanish court, secured the dismissal of the governor (as they did once again in Florida and several times in New Mexico) and returned to evangelism with renewed vigor. Within a few years they claimed 26,000 Indian converts, and seventy friars were operating forty thriving missions. Modern skeptics have reduced these exuberant numbers, but the king was pleased. The truth, though more modest, was grand enough.

Recent archaeological discoveries have permitted us to reconstruct the appearance of some of these missions. The first Indian converts were too numerous to be assembled in the church buildings. Though some sanctuaries were as much as one hundred feet long, they seem to have been intended only for the garrison and the clergy. But the "open chapel" tradition was maintained by creating large, level plazas. They appear to have been used in the same way as those of Yucatán, at the other extreme of the Spanish endeavors in the Caribbean.

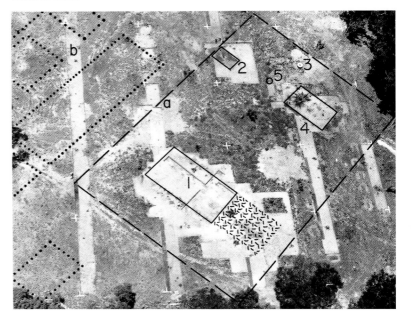

Above:
Archaeology on an airfield: the layout of Mission Santa Catalina de Guale and its associated pueblo on Saint Catherines Island, superimposed on the modern site. The church is (1), the convento (4), and the kitchen (2); the wall is the rectangle marked (a); the pueblo was at the blocks marked (b).

These churches were not so long and thin as those of the Franciscans in Mexico and the Southwest; their proportions were usually two in length for one in width rather than four (or more) to one, as was common in the West. Some may have been constructed of stockade-like uprights laid on a sill, but most seem to have been built of wattle and daub like that used by peasants in Spain and North Africa. Small buildings (conventos) were divided into tiny cells to house the Franciscans; granaries and farm buildings surrounded most plazas.

Architectural historians delight in debating whether these plazas demonstrate deference to the mound-bounded plazas already licensed by centuries of tradition among the Indians represent a triumph of Renaissance tidiness over the spontaneity of Moorish town planning. Central plazas *were* beginning to be built in the new cities of Ferdinand and Isabella as Columbus set sail. My own hunch is that the plazas served at once as open chapels, as consoling modes of ordering a threatening and exotic landscape, as locations for the rapid deployment of troops to stand off casual attack, and as means to bring the Indians into spaces they might find familiar and thus "welcoming" in a British sense.

Such solicitousness did not seem important at first, either in Florida or in New Mexico. But the Pueblo Revolt of 1680 repeated the signal given by the Apalachee Revolt of 1647. Thereafter the Spanish authorities bought acquiescence to their suzerainty by assuring the Indians that their religious and architectural preferences would be, to a considerable extent, respected.

Circular kivas have been found within the precincts of some of the New Mexican missions. Some may have been there before the Pueblo Revolt; some may have been built as symbols of rejection of the Spaniards' religion during the independence of Native American New Mexico from 1680 to 1692. It would have been an elegant symbol of accommodative evangelicalism if some were permitted, even after the Spanish return, to function, euphemistically, as council houses. Perhaps something similar happened earlier in Florida. Many eyewitnesses, including Bishop Gabriel Diaz Vara Calderón in 1674, reported that in many missions the parishioners gathered in round council houses (*buhios*) like those that had been the tribes' community centers before Europeans arrived. Perhaps in some circumstances they merely continued to use the same structures. The *buhios* were very large; Calderón said some could house 2,000 to 3,000 people, and there is archaeological evidence of *buhios* nearly 140 feet in diameter. They seem to have been open at the top in the center, with walls and sloped ceilings made of wood covered by thatch or straw.

Their interior walls were painted with murals. One account by a Spaniard of a Timacuan council house speaks of "battles and histories painted with great naturalness." As late as the end of the eighteenth century, the naturalist William Bartram wrote of Creek murals representing "many forms of animal

and plant life." The buildings described by Bartram probably went to the flames of Andrew Jackson's invaders after 1819; those of the Timacua had disappeared considerably earlier.

By 1600 the French had withdrawn to the West Indies, Louisiana, and Canada. Though the Spaniards still had to fight little wars with them in Texas and had to build missions there to stand them off, Spanish Jesuits met French Jesuits in the corridors of the Vatican and came to understandings.

Britain, however, had joined Holland among the Protestant powers. English and Dutch pirates prowled the Caribbean, and after the founding of Charles Town (Charleston) in 1670, Britain proclaimed itself the antagonist of Spain along the northern fringes of Florida.

Hostilities began in earnest in 1680, as English-armed Creeks, Cherokees, and Chiscas attacked the Christianized Guales and the Spaniards at the mission Santiago de Ocono on Jekyll Island. By 1700 nothing was left of the missions on the Florida shore. In 1702, Santa Fe in Timacuan territory was burned out by the British and their Indian allies, the first of the missions in the interior to go up in flames. The following May, James Moore, the slave-trading governor of Carolina, led his Indians and frontiersmen against St. Augustine. Though he managed to burn all the churches in the town, the Castel San Marcos could not be taken, and the cattle driven into its dry moat survived. The church at Nombre de Dios (where Menéndez had come ashore) was built of coquina limestone, and it seems to have resisted Moore's torches as well.

Moore did not at first assault the remaining island missions. But when their time came in 1705, the English spared nothing. The chapels were made of wood or inflammable wattle and daub; their roofs were thatch, their defenses mere stockades. Though resistance was fierce, Moore completed his project of "intirely kniving all the Indian towns in Florida." On an official map a legend was written across the region where once had stood forty thriving missions: "Wholly Laid Waste Being Destroyed by the Carolinians, 1706."

What happened to the people? If one wishes to know how an apocalypse may be compressed into the flat, bleached language of social science, this is the response to that question recently given by a team of archaeologists: "Periodic food shortages, reduced dietary diversity, loss of valuable stored foods, European-introduced diseases, increased work demand, retaliation by the military following native uprisings, and pressure from the English-occupied regions to the north — resulted in the decline and eventual extinction of these populations." A Crusade with no survivors.

What is meant by "increased work demand"? One supply train from the Apalachee missions to St. Augustine returned with only ten out of one hundred Indian bearers. "Pressure"? Three thousand Indians died in battles with Moore's troops in the Apalachee lands alone, fighting beside the warrior-priest Juan de Parga. If we accept the Spanish figure of 25,000 parishioners at the beginning and assume that 90 percent of the population had already died of disease by the sixteenth century, then a reduction of these 25,000 to none at all does indeed complete a considerable "decline."

It is possible that some of the Guale, Timacua, and Apalachee escaped into the unconquered lands of central Florida and eventually assimilated into the refugee people called "Seminole." Others may have gone north and west to live among the Cherokee, Choctaw, or the Muskogee, called by the English "Creek." At the end of Spanish rule in the nineteenth century, south-central Florida was still held by people never conquered and never Christianized, descendants of the Calusa. They were masters of small-boat naval warfare amid the swamps and estuaries; for over three centuries they demonstrated themselves to be as fierce as the Hopi of the high desert Southwest.

Strong immune systems may have saved the Calusa from extinction by European or African diseases. Other immunities, of an intellectual variety, kept them from being attracted to European agriculture, from being compressed into plague-swept villages, and from demoralization. Perhaps their greatest good fortune was that they were at some remove from the English and not living on the fertile and accessible corn lands that had attracted both the Spaniards and the English to the low hills of the Apalachee.

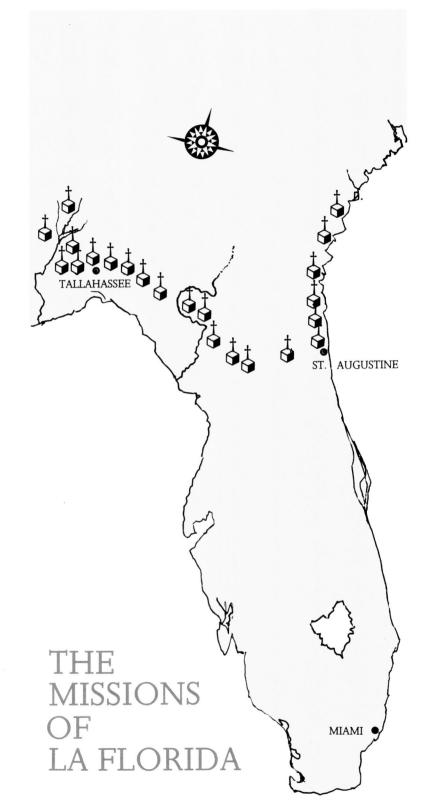

TALLAHASSEE

ST. AUGUSTINE

MIAMI

THE
MISSIONS
OF
LA FLORIDA

SONORA AND ITS COLONIES, CALIFORNIA AND ARIZONA

FATHER EUSEBIO FRANCISCO KINO (1645–1711) was an evangelist of irresistible persuasiveness. He was also a gifted geographer and statesman and an indefatigable explorer. He was the first to demonstrate to European satisfaction that Baja California was a peninsula rather than an island. As a founder of missions, Kino was constantly in the saddle, always impatient for a new valley, a new range of mountains, a new river, a new congregation to bring to his savior.

Padre Kino, from the Tyrol, was in modern terms Italian, as were many of his chief associates in laying the bases for missions in Arizona and California. On the east coast of Baja California, Fathers Francisco Maria Piccolo and Giuseppe María Salvatierra organized a cluster of four missions between 1697 and 1701. (Multinationality expressed itself in a variety of ways on the Spanish frontier: most of the Italian-originated missions of Baja were destroyed by a rising of 1734, in which the Indians were joined by descendants of English and Dutch pirates and of crew members of those Manila galleons that had paused for replenishment and recreation on the coast.)

Kino's early mission did not try to provide the Arizona Indians with resident clergy. His churches were small, designed for visiting priests, not continuous residence; none of them survive, either north or south of the present international border. (That border, purely artificial geographically and sociologically, cuts brutally across Kino's theater of operations and makes it very difficult for us to consider that terrain as the continuity it was both to the Indians and to the Catholic missionaries.)

As Father Charles Polzer has made clear, there are no "Kino churches" to be visited today, though hundreds of people make pilgrimages to seek them out, both in Arizona and in northern Mexico. The buildings that exist now were created at or near places selected by Kino, but the actual structures were built after his death. Even more poignantly, they were constructed after the Spanish Empire's violent expulsion of the Jesuit order in 1767.

That event, staggering in its consequences for the entire mission enterprise, occurred as Europe crystallized into modern nation states. Imperial monarchs ceased to be willing to tolerate within their realms powerful organizations whose primary allegiance was to Rome. The Society of Jesus, though formed after the onset of the Renaissance, was the final flowering of the supranational medieval church. Even at the extremities of the European empires, the Jesuits' presence slowly became intolerable to kings. In 1767, in Arizona, Baja California, Texas, and Florida, soldiers of the Crown swept down upon isolated missions, arrested the Jesuits, and in many instances pressed them into forced marches toward concentration camps. The survivors went into exile.

The expulsion of the Jesuits occurred as a resurgence of Spanish energy startled Europe on many fronts. It had become a habit for other nations to disparage Spain as exhausted and faintly foolish. The British Empire was ascendant from Malacca to Buenos Aires and Vancouver; France, though forced to relinquish Canada and Louisiana after 1763, was still formidable; Frederick the Great had disciplined Prussia into the Sparta of Europe; Austria had driven off the Ottomans; and Russia was a looming presence of incalculable potentiality. As these powers rose, Spain seemed, if not the "sick man of Europe," then the old man of Europe.

While the Atlantic world was convulsed by these changes, Spain suddenly came alive again toward the end of the eighteenth century and created upon the northern horizon of its American empire the picturesque missions of Texas and California, which for Americans are the most accessible examples of its missionary activity. They were no longer expressions of a continuous missionary urgency, but instead, statements of an apprehensive aggression, intended as much to stave off European competitors as to convert Indians.

In Florida these purposes had been coincident all along, and they became more intensely conjoined after the first French and British attacks. Both objectives had failed. By 1710 the mission system was withdrawn from the southeastern frontier, and when the United States extinguished the Spanish Empire in North America a little more than a century later, it was simply playing out the British hand.

In the West the story was somewhat more complicated. The multinational expansion of Catholic Europe, directed by Spain, brought missionaries and garrisons to staging areas in northwestern Mexico from which they then proceeded into Arizona and then California. The first priests to reside in Arizona in the spring of 1732 were German Jesuits. The first pastor at San Xavier del Bac was Philip Segesser von Brunegg; at Guevavi, Johann Grazhofer; at Soamca, Ignatz Keller. Twenty years later, after the Pima had risen, Segesser, now joined by Gaspar Stiger and Jacobo Sedelmayr, were sufficiently expert in secular as well as religious matters that the governor of Sonora asked their judgment as to where troops should be stationed. As a result of this Sud-Deutsch consortium, the first permanent European settlement in Arizona was created around a new presidio at Tubac.

In Baja California, the great Jesuit names of the eighteenth century included Bischoff, Wagner, Gasteiger, Hostell, Retz, Ducrue, Inama, Baegert, and Tempis. Ferdinand Consag, a Croatian, moved out of this central European enclave to explore upper California, followed by a Bohemian, Wenceslaus Linck.

Opposite: The belfry at Caborca.

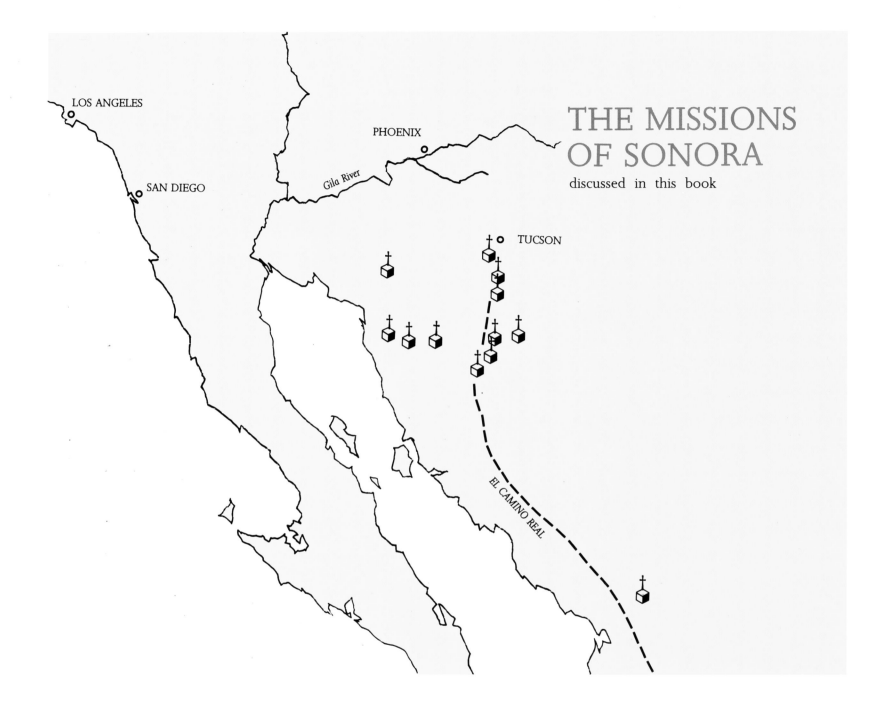

THE MISSIONS OF SONORA

discussed in this book

LOS ANGELES

SAN DIEGO

PHOENIX

Gila River

TUCSON

EL CAMINO REAL

Opposite: The Roman church, part of the ancient Mediterranean world, reached into the ancient American world and created buildings worthy of Palmyra, Leptis Magna, or Baalbek. These are the ruins of the church of Nuestra Señora del Pilar y Santiago de Cocóspera in Sonora; the shell of a Franciscan church surrounds a large Jesuit church founded by Father Kino.

Father Bernard Middendorff became the first resident priest in Tucson in January 1757. Segesser's sense that the burdens of expanding the "Spanish" presence was falling largely upon non-Spanish priests was seconded by Father Ignaz Pfefferkorn, who wrote that "besides the governor of Sonora, the officers of the Spanish garrisons, and a few merchants . . . there is hardly a true Spaniard in Sonora." (Sonora at that time included Arizona as well as the much more densely and safely settled region of northern Mexico.)

The following is a working list of the Franciscan churches built on Jesuit sites in present-day Sonora and Arizona.
Below:
In Sonora, Nuestra Señora del Pilar y Santiago de Cocóspera (on the north side of the highway between Imuris and Cananea) is a grand ruin, accumulated from Kino's Jesuit church of 1698, its Jesuit replacement of 1704 after destruction by the Apache, and a Franciscan renewal after 1776. It is imperiled by wind, weather, and time.

Above:

San Ignacio de Caburica (six miles north of Magdalena de Kino) is the latest of a series of churches built on a site selected by Kino in 1687 in an existing Indian ranchería. It is possible that this is the structure built by the German Jesuit Gaspar Stiger in 1753 on the ruins of a Jesuit precursor destroyed several times, initially by a Pima revolt in 1695. More likely the present church was built by the Franciscan friar Francisco Sanchez Zuniga in the 1770s. It has escaped the dynamiters and filibusters and remains in wonderful condition, only a little remodeled.

San Pedro y San Pablo del Tubutama in Sonora lies about forty miles from Highway 2 and eight miles from Atil on Highway 64, on a turnoff requiring a side trip of a mile and a half to the east. Father Kino began building a church here in 1687; the present church was built by Franciscans in 1788.

San Antonio del Oquitoa (just upriver from Altar) was a Jesuit mission named for a Franciscan saint. In the opinion of Bernard Fontana, the church itself is probably the Jesuit structure, dating as far back as the 1740s; the facade, added by Franciscans, was heavily restored in 1980.

Right: The full panoply of Mediterranean classicism — scalloped doorway, engaged columns, niches for statuary — is arrayed on the facade.

Left: The nave and altar at San Ignacio de Caburica.

Above:
San Diego del Pitiquito (in Pitiquin, west of Altar) was built in
1778 and remodeled frequently thereafter.

In Arizona, both San Xavier and the partially ruined San José de Tumacácori are statements of Jesuit intention and Franciscan accomplishment. San Xavier, seven miles south and two miles west of Tucson off Interstate 19, is a functioning parish church, as alive today as when it was completed in 1797. Tumacácori is forty-eight miles to the south off the same highway. It was begun in 1802, but construction was broken off in 1822, and the church was abandoned in 1848. After heavy restoration it is now a museum managed by the National Park Service.

San José de Tumacácori.

Above: A rattlesnake and its prey latch the door of San Xavier del Bac.

Opposite: Interrupted work: vestiges of plaster ornament in San José de Tumacácori, left incomplete when Pima parishioners were forced away by Apache raids in 1848.

The mission and its consequences, both wonderful and terrible, are represented in the retablo at San Xavier del Bac, outside Tucson.

Opposite: The sanctuary at San Xavier del Bac has the most complete surviving ornament and fixtures of any mission church in the United States.

San José de Gracia at Trampas, New Mexico, completed about 1763.

THE RIO GRANDE

THOUGH WE HAVE BECOME ACCUSTOMED to thinking of the Rio Grande as part of the southern border of the United States, historically its chief significance has been as a river running from north to south. That is its course before it turns southeasterly to distinguish Texas from Mexico on maps. Because of its orientation, the river corridor has more often served as an invasion route than as a barrier. Traveling upstream from the Gulf of Mexico, through interminable greasewood plains, one traverses the canyon of the Big Bend around the Davis Mountains and then heads roughly northward for seven hundred miles toward the Rockies.

The unexpectedness of the history of the Spanish borderlands commences characteristically with the fact that the first Europeans to reach the Rio Grande were a black man and a white man, neither of whom intended to be there and who came from Florida. Estavanico, a Moor, and a Spanish companion were the survivors of the *entrada* of Pánfilo de Narvaéz against the Florida coast in 1528. They walked, rowed, and staggered all the way across the Gulf plain and into Texas. Baffled by the confusing course of the Rio Grande, they headed north in search of food and friendly Indians. Having crossed a thousand miles of desert, they were picking their way down the Pacific slope when, barefoot and clothed only in loincloths, they came upon a slaving party of Spaniards sent out from the advance posts of the suzerainty of Cortés. After some wary inspection, they were welcomed and debriefed.

Riches had come easily to Cortés and his lieutenants. So many rivals of the Aztecs were willing to ally themselves with the Europeans and lead them to further spoils that these rational men assumed that more valleys of gold lay just beyond every horizon. Slaving was a means to pick up a little spending money while they reconnoitered these new bonanzas.

Meanwhile the Church was seeking to save souls and to protect those already entrusted to it by preventing the worst cruelties of the soldiers, slavers, and miners. After the great building program of the middle of the sixteenth century in the valley of Mexico, missionary activity spread northward up the Rio Grande.

Right: Nuestra Señora de la Asunción at Zia Pueblo, New Mexico; begun about 1614, the church was rebuilt several times, but part of the structure may be original. The bell tower takes the form of the traditional Anasazi cloud motif, associated with the powers of the heavens.

NEW MEXICO

Francisco Vásquez de Coronado's expeditionary force had nothing to do with saving souls. His object was as uncomplicated as that of his English counterparts Richard Hawkins, Francis Drake, and Thomas Cavendish. The only difference among them was that the English went after swag at sea. For Coronado, silver would *do*, but gold was the true prize, drawing him on through sagebrush, sand dunes, snow, and slush, past dusty pueblos and stampeding buffalo herds, away from the Rio Grande and in 1543 out into the interminable short-grass prairie of Nebraska. One can imagine how deep was the disgust arising from his disappointed avarice.

A half century later Catholic Europe did establish an advance base on the upper Rio Grande. St. Augustine in Florida had been founded in 1565. (Because Santa Fe was not made the capital of its desolate province until 1609, Jamestown takes second place to St. Augustine among continuously occupied European settlements in America. Such Indian villages as Oriabe and Acoma had been settled for seven centuries longer, and are still.)

The story of the New Mexico missions is fairly familiar. A capsule summary of what may be seen at each of those that still survives may give a sense of what was there in the seventeenth century.

Of all the New Mexico mission churches, only San Esteban del Rey de Acoma, on the top of the butte at Acoma, remains almost as it has always been. The church, fifty-two miles west of Albuquerque, is open to controlled public visits. Built between 1629 and 1641, it was abandoned during the Pueblo Revolt (1680–1692) but has otherwise been in continuous use.

Right: The mesa, village, and church at Acoma.

Ruins, some partially restored or "stabilized" but all picturesque and evocative, are to be found at Pecos, Quarai (a nearly complete but abandoned mission eight miles northwest of Mountainair), San Gregorio de Abó (off Interstate 25 at Bernardo), Gran Quivira (twenty-five miles southeast of Mountainair), and Jemez Springs (off State Highway 44 forty-two miles northwest of Bernalillo). These were all built in the seventeenth century.

The following missions have been restored and are in use for the purpose for which they were established nearly four centuries ago:

Nuestra Señora de la Asunción de Zia (twenty miles northwest of Bernalillo at Zia Pueblo) is a partially restored structure that dates back to 1706. There was some reconstruction in the late eighteenth or early nineteenth century.

Nuestra Señora de Guadalupe de Zuñi is forty miles southwest of Gallup at Zuñi Pueblo. Construction on the church began around 1699 and was restored in 1969.

San Agustín de la Isleta is thirteen miles south of Albuquerque off Interstate 25. Some remodeling has been done, but portions of the church date from 1613. Isleta vies with Acoma for the distinction of being the oldest church in New Mexico; probably more of the old church at Acoma is still intact. (The claims of San Miguel Chapel in Santa Fe to be the oldest church are not supported by evidence; it dates from 1709–10.)

The present church at San Buenaventura de Cochiti (twenty-four miles northwest of Bernalillo off Interstate 25) was completed in the eighteenth century.

San Felipe (thirty-five miles southwest of Santa Fe near the San Felipe Pueblo) dates to 1736. The church has had very few alterations.

San José de Laguna (forty-five miles west of Albuquerque, off Interstate 40 at Laguna Pueblo) was built in 1706. The only major change was an interior whitewashing in 1968, which covered a painted wall.

San Lorenzo de Picurís (twenty miles south of Taos at Picurís Pueblo) dates to 1776. It is in danger of collapse, and several retablos have been removed for protection.

San Miguel Socorro (seventy-seven miles west of Albuquerque) was originally called Nuestra Señora de Perpetuo Socorro. Something may be left of the seventeenth-century structure, which was abandoned from 1680 until the 1820s and then completely rebuilt. It was renovated in 1973.

The church at Santa Ana Pueblo (twelve miles northwest of Bernalillo, off State Highway 44) was completed by 1734. The site is well maintained.

The following churches have been rebuilt, perhaps similarly to the original:

San Ildefonso (three miles north of State Highway 126 near Los Alamos), completed in 1968, is a good reproduction of the 1711 church.

The original church at Santo Domingo Pueblo (west of Interstate 25, off State Highway 22) was destroyed in the Pueblo Revolt of 1680. The present church was built about 1895.

Opposite: The ruined mission church of Nuestra Señora de la Purísima Concepción de Quarai in New Mexico.
The church at Quarai was begun about 1628, using heavily buttressed stone. The roof was still in place in 1853. The structure has been stabilized and is in the care of the National Park Service.

Above: Christmas Eve *luminarias* at St. Esteban del Rey de Acoma, New Mexico. *Opposite:* One of the bells at the church. The rhythms of life at Acoma have reached an accommodation with the rhythms of the clock.

The ruins of San Gregorio de Abó, in Salinas Pueblo Missions National Monument.

Opposite: Ruins of San José de Jemez, Jemez State Monument, New Mexico. Note the tower behind the high altar, protecting the sanctuary from the hill above.

San Agustin de la Isleta, New Mexico; portions of the fabric of
the sanctuary go back to 1613. Along with the church at Acoma,
it is the oldest church still in service in the United States.

San José at Laguna Pueblo, New Mexico, in the snow.

San José at Laguna Pueblo. Whitewash has obliterated the original decorations on the exterior walls.

The Gothic spirit persisted as late as 1709 in the tower of San Miguel Chapel in Santa Fe, New Mexico.

The Mediterranean influence, with Maltese crosses, is shown on the doors of the church at Santa Cruz, New Mexico.

Entering the walled cemetery of the Santuario del Señor de Esquipulas at Chimayo, New Mexico.

The retablo at the busy Santuario de Chimayo.

Cement protects adobe at the church at Abiquiu, New Mexico.

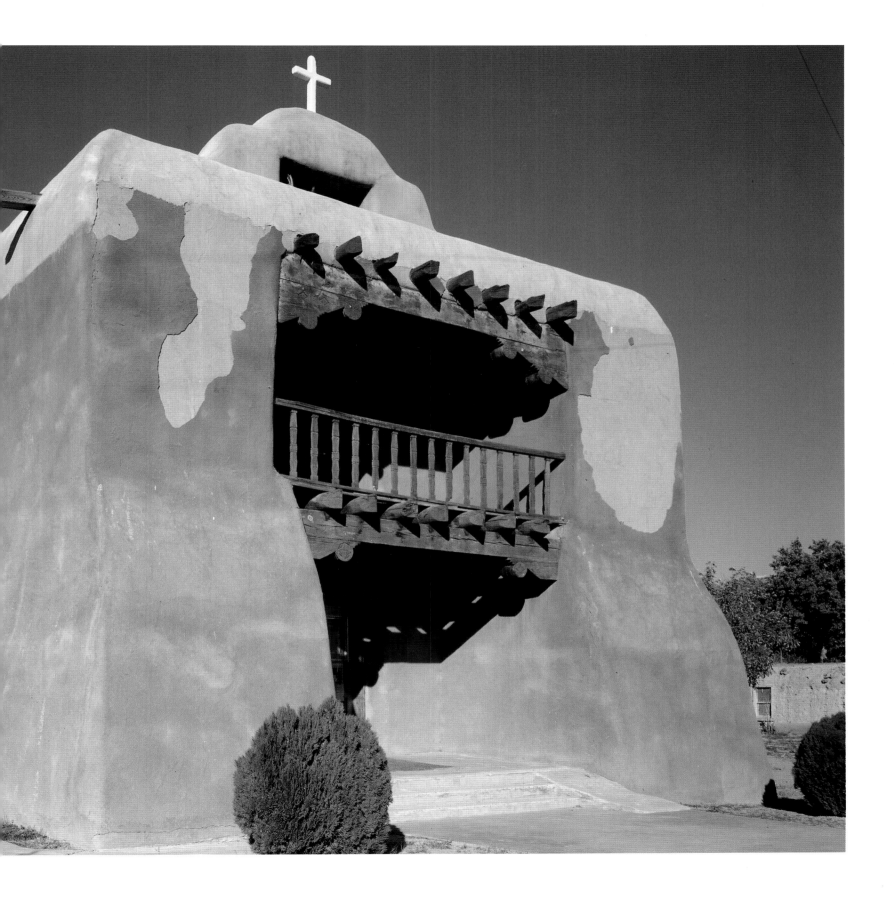

San José de Gracia at Trampas, New Mexico: the exterior choir loft permits accompaniment as processionals move out of the church into the community.

155

The church of San Geronimo at Taos Pueblo.

The church at San Ildefonso Pueblo.

Opposite: The adobe abutment made famous in the paintings of Georgia O'Keeffe, supporting the sanctuary wall of the church of Saint Francis at Ranchos de Taos.

TEXAS

After the survivors of Narváez's *entrada* had disappeared across the western horizon, the inhabitants of Texas were left almost undisturbed by Europeans until René-Robert Cavelier, sieur de La Salle, built a fort on the coast and named it for Saint Louis, the same Crusader king of France commemorated at San Luis Rey in California. La Salle was a Norman knight who had already established one fort, at Starved Rock in Illinois, in the militant memory of Louis IX (who had acquired uncontested possession of Normandy from the English kings). The empire of Louis XIV, no saint, was in its expansionary phase, and La Salle's presence sent tremors all the way to Madrid.

Spain's response was its customary combination of missionary zeal and geopolitical policy. Expectations of a rich kingdom of the Tejes had languished for eighty years, but the silver mines of San Luis Potosí in Mexico were producing in profusion. Texas, even a squalid and unprofitable Texas, could act as a buffer between the mines and La Salle. In the seventeenth century the lower reaches of the Rio Grande Valley were being settled, and missionary fervor of the New Mexican variety produced tales of a mysterious "Lady in Blue," a nun who was at work saving souls among the Indians far in advance of the military.

After La Salle placed his standard upon Texas soil, four Spanish expeditions made their way along its coast, and five overland explorations penetrated inland from bases along the Rio Grande. They found the charred and pillaged remains of Fort Saint Louis, the skeletons of its garrison, and a scene of Indian revenge. Mass was said over the bones, and the Spaniards departed. Later two French boys who had been spared were found living among the Indians. In 1690 two small missions were established along the Neches River. The fringes of Florida had been colonized for 130 years. Though the British threat was increasing, there was no doubt in Madrid of the value of the peninsula, in combination with Havana, in protecting the homeward route of the silver ships. New Mexico caused little trouble, though one could never tell when the Apaches, now in possession of both firearms and horses, might gather to imperil the northern defenses of the Mexican sources of that silver. The French might be worrisome, but Louis XIV was facing surprising opposition in Europe from the great captains Marlborough and Prince Eugène of Savoy, and it seemed unlikely that he would

bother much with squalid Texas, even as a route to San Luis Potosí.

So, despite protests from the Franciscans, who persisted in thinking that salvation should have some role in these calculations, the first Spanish missions in Texas were withdrawn. Indian religious practices remained undisturbed until the French did a very strange thing: they turned Louisiana over to private enterprise. Tiring of the expense and embarrassment of attempting to make distant Louisiana economically healthy by state-managed means, the court of Versailles handed it to Antoine Crozat. Crozat, in turn, delegated his entrepreneurship to Antoine de La Mothe, sieur de Cadillac. (Auto lovers may be pleased to know that Cadillac made his way to the lower Mississippi from Detroit, entering terrain already known to de Soto, La Salle, and the Cherokee.)

Cadillac renewed commercial intrusions on the Texas borderland and in 1714 sent out Jean Juchereau de Saint-Denis toward the Rio Grande and toward a celebrated intra-European romance of the missions. Saint-Denis was the successful suitor of Doña Emanuela, niece of the commander of the first large-scale Spanish mission and presidio into which he wandered, San Juan Bautista, on the south bank of the Rio Grande, north of Laredo.

There is no way of assessing whether Saint-Denis's intentions were honorable; he was a charmer, she loved him, his circumstances were perilous, and he married her. Though he stayed in touch with Cadillac, he assumed the role of a soldier of Spain; the mystery is whether he was a double agent or merely a realist in politics as well as romance.

Saint-Denis and Doña Emanuela's father were soon leading the first permanent Spanish settlers into Texas. They were accompanied by a group of Franciscans from the college of Querétaro, who had one architectural tradition, and a second group from Zacatecas, who had another. The *Te Deum* was sung and four missions established in East Texas between the Trinity and the Neches rivers — in modern terms, close to the Louisiana-Texas border. The French were already garrisoning Natchitoches (named for one son of a local chieftain); the Spaniards dug themselves in at Nacogdoches (named for the other son).

In 1719 these hostile and competitive Europeans came to blows. Eight French soldiers sent the Spanish missionaries at San Miguel de los Adaes packing. The Spaniards acquiesced but began storing military supplies and raising troops. The presidio and missions at San Antonio were by now in place; from there a Spanish army set forth against the French and their Indian allies in May 1721. Despite the efforts of Saint-Denis, once more wearing the colors of France, the leader of the Spanish army could not be dissuaded from reinstalling a presence in East Texas.

By the end of the following year, ten mission-garrisons were in place and two new fortresses had been established. French Jesuits competed with Spanish Franciscans for the souls of the Indians; Spanish and French merchants competed for Indian goods. Spanish and French army recruiters competed, offering horses and firearms in return for service. Silver was actually discovered in Texas, and in the 1750s a new mission, San Saba, was established to guard it.

By this time, however, the Comanche had developed military technology, tactics, and a capacity for coordinated campaigns that made them as formidable as any European cavalry. While they were acquiring these skills, they had been vulnerable to Spanish attack and had learned bitter lessons. Now they assaulted the Spanish outposts with a competence and fury that made the French seem torpid in comparison. Two thousand Comanche burned out the environs of San Saba, assassinated friars, and drove off herds of horses. In 1759 a major Spanish expeditionary force paraded northward into hostile territory. Near the present town of Ringgold, Texas, they came upon a fortified village garrisoned by Indians but flying the French flag. The Spanish tried artillery, but the defenders had learned about that as well, and their defenses held. As the Spanish attackers grew weary and discouraged, the Comanche sortied and drove them from the field. Things were changing on the plains, as they had changed in Natchez in 1729, when for the first time Indian forces under their own command took a European fort by sustained siege. The French lost their garrison at Fort Rosalie (Natchez), and though their vengeance was so terrible that the Natchez nation ceased to exist, the lesson of European invincibility was being unlearned, and the West made ready for Pontiac and Tecumseh, Little Crow and Red Cloud.

In the missions, however, safely behind the lines, life went on. Here is a short summary of what modern visitors may

expect to find at the remaining missions of Texas to remind them of what that life was like.

La Purísima de Socorro (eighteen miles southeast of El Paso) was built in 1842, with a transept added in 1876. The mission was originally established in Socorro, New Mexico; it was moved to Texas after the Pueblo Revolt in 1680 and moved several times thereafter. The church has been partly restored or reconstructed.

Nuestra Señora de la Purísima Concepción de Acuña (three miles southwest of downtown San Antonio on Mission Road) was built in 1739. Traces of the original frescoes secco remain.

San Antonio de Valero (the Alamo), in downtown San Antonio, was begun in 1744. It collapsed in 1748. Rebuilding commenced in 1756 but was never completed. In the nineteenth century an imaginative upper portion of facade was added to cover the front of a pitched roof built to cover quartermaster storage. The new roof is close to the original but without a dome. Other improvements have been made to the building, now a museum.

San Juan Capistrano (San Antonio) was established in 1731; the convent building is now offices and a museum. One of the granaries was converted into the present church.

San Francisco de la Espada (San Antonio, a mile south of San Juan Capistrano on Espada Road) was commenced about 1744 as a sacristy for a larger church. It was modified in 1780, 1831, and the 1950s. Today it is a museum.

The church of San José y San Miguel de Aguayo (San Antonio, two miles south of Mission Concepción) was built in the 1720s and incorporated into a larger church in 1768. It has been magnificently restored and is part of a museum complex.

The Mission Espiritu Santo complex at Goliad (southeast of San Antonio), is now part of Goliad State Park. The buildings have been reconstructed, along with the presidio compound and a chapel.

Above and opposite: San José y San Miguel de Aguayo, San Antonio, Texas, was begun in the 1720s and incorporated into a larger church in the 1760s. It is now a magnificently restored museum complex.

Above and opposite: San Francisco de la Espada, San Antonio, Texas, was begun about 1744. It was heavily restored in the 1950s.

ELEV +22'-9¾" ELEV +24-1½"

LEAD ROOF

ELEV. - 4" ELEV. +8"

ORIGINAL MISSION WALLS EXTEND TO DOTTED LINE; THIS ELEVATION STUCCOED & PAINTED
ALL WINDOWS THIS ELEVATION CUT THROUGH c. 1847-1848.

~ SOUTH~ELEVATION ~

SCALE : 1/8" = 1'-0"

LEAD ROOF

ELEV +22'-5¼" ELEV + 22'-7½"

WALL ADDED 1847-1848

TOWER DOOR

ORIGINAL LIME-
STONE WALL

SEALED
OPENINGS

ELEV + 1'- 7½"

NEW WORK ABOVE DOTTED LINE. EXCEPT FOR ORIGINAL TOWER DOOR; ALL OPENINGS CUT c. 1847-1848.

~ NORTH~ELEVATION ~

SCALE : 1/8" = 1'-0"

JAMES EMMRICH, DEL.

0 5 10 15 20
SCALE IN FEET
0 1 2 3 4 5 6 7 8 9 10
SCALE IN VARAS
0 1 2 3 4 5 6 7 8 9 10
SCALE IN METERS

Above: A HABS drawing of the Alamo (the mission church of San Antonio de Valero) in San Antonio, Texas.

Opposite: The Alamo, begun in 1744, was begun again in 1756 but left unfinished. It was a shell when occupied by Texans during the famous siege in 1836.

166

Nuestra Señora de la Purísima Concepción de Acuña

THE CALIFORNIAS

THE TOPOGRAPHY ACROSS WHICH EUROPE approached the Californias is unambiguous; unlike that of the southeastern United States, the terrain of Sonora and Sinaloa leaves few options for locations of settlement or the sequence of missionary activity. Deep canyons run in parallel southwesterly from the Sierra Madres into the Gulf of California. Some of these canyons of Mexico are as deep as the Grand Canyon of the Colorado. Seen from a Mexican perspective, *that* famous tourist attraction is merely the last and longest of these impediments. For those trying to get to California the Grand Canyon was conveniently out of the way. (There was nothing to recommend crossing the Colorado River in its canyon, for until the Mormons colonized both banks, it was seen as merely an interruption of the desert. Near its mouth it is the only one of this succession of rivers to have a delta of sufficient size to permit a train of animals or settlers to move easily from one bank to the other.)

Along the eastern shore of the Gulf of California, where the canyons ended, Spanish energy eddied. Missionaries first set themselves up in temporary shelters, then created fortified buildings of increasing ambition at widenings in the canyon floors where Indians were growing maize, beans, and cotton. Next they reconnoitered ways to cross each canyon, assault each next ridge, and repeat the process in the next canyon. Prodigies of church building still remain in these remote and isolated places.

At the same time the barren peninsula of Baja was being colonized by Spanish, Flemish, and German Jesuits, succeeded by Dominicans. It was as difficult as it had been in central Mexico to sustain the illusion that the inhabitants were mere savages. Though the land is harsh, their artistic accomplishments were of a size so astonishing and were of such an antiquity that even the most xenophobic of the Europeans admitted to awe. Huge rock-art figures are still encountered in remote places in Baja; those who come upon them, still astonishing and still untended, are dazzled. What must have been their effects upon churchmen unprepared for anything on this scale?

FROM DRAKE TO CAPTAIN COOK

The missions of New Mexico and Arizona had little or no geopolitical purpose. Other European empires presented no threat to the central section of the northern frontier of New Spain. A few French traders straggled into Pecos, but it was not until after 1803, when Thomas Jefferson followed the Louisiana Purchase with a series of probes of the defenses of Mexico, that there was anything to fear from the north and east.

California and Texas, however, on either flank of Mexico's northern defenses, were thought to be threatened by other European contenders from the outset. As soon as their Protestant queen, Elizabeth, was firmly in possession of the throne of England, British freebooters started making raids on Spanish shipping in the Caribbean. These were followed by fleets of twenty or more vessels carrying amphibious forces. Full-scale assaults were launched upon Signor Antonelli's fortresses at Cartagena, Havana, and Portobelo, within which reposed gold and silver wrested from the Indians and awaiting transfer to Europe. Sir Francis Drake commanded the most formidable and successful of these expeditions.

Drake's outrages were capped by his impertinence in rounding the southern tip of Spain's New World empire and appearing in the Pacific, which, for a few decades after first being glimpsed by Balboa and traversed by Magellan, had been a Spanish lake. The Philippines had been found and named for Philip II. The Manila galleons carried Mexican silver to the Far East and returned with the Oriental luxuries that had drawn Columbus toward the West to start with. Despite the intervention of a continent, an extra ocean, and a half century, the dream of Isabella seemed nearly fulfilled — until Drake appeared off the coast of California.

He reached there after raiding surprised and undefended settlements all the way from Chile to the tip of Baja. News traveled very slowly up the coast; none of the Spanish colonial garrisons were warned of his approach. It is unlikely that word of his ravages actually reached Spain itself from the colonies until the Jesuit secret service brought word from London that Drake was reporting appetizing opportunities to the queen, his sovereign and partner.

The Spanish ministers pondered the possibility of preempting British bases on the west coast of America. Expeditions were sent northward from Baja and Sonora and northwestward into the desert from Arizona and New Mexico to search for routes to California. Having demonstrated the extreme poverty of the intervening land and the presence of daunting canyons and deserts, the expeditions returned.
For two centuries British sails occasionally appeared on the Pacific horizon; in the 1740s a new generation of privateers — licensed pirates — pillaged the ports of Peru and captured galleons off Manila, and in 1762 that westernmost of Spanish possessions was taken — though it was returned in a subsequent treaty.

Whenever the British threat seemed to subside, so, too, did the ardor of the Spanish Crown for subsidizing advance posts. But by the end of the eighteenth century the creole elite of Mexico itself was becoming philanthropic and full of both missionary zeal and apprehensions about the British. They themselves organized a society to subsidize mission-garrisons on their northern frontier to supplement what might be offered by the Crown.

The scarlet peril was renewed by the highly publicized voyages of Captain Cook in the 1770s. By this time a new contender had appeared. The Russians had come upon their own "peak of Darien," "discovering" the Pacific from the west in 1639. They promptly entered the competition for both shores of that opulent basin, which, after all, had witnessed the movement of humankind from west to east long before either Britain or Spain was civilized. The Empress Catherine the Great made known her disdain for the pretensions of Spain; Russian trappers and traders had pressed down the American Pacific coast by the time Cook made his appearance offshore.

Crisscrossing claims were sketched across the map of the North Pacific. The Russians hunted seals in San Francisco Bay from their entrepôt at Bodega Bay, not far to the north, and their stockade at Fort Ross (for Rossia). The Spaniards' riposte was a foray into Alaskan waters. In the 1730s and 1740s the Russians began publishing appetizing accounts of the silver wealth of Mexico, accompanied by righteous indignation about the Spaniards' treatment of the Indians (they expressed no matching fervor in the interest of the Alaskan aborigines). The Russian fascination intensified in the 1770s; one Ivan Krylov commenced writing an opera called *Amerikantsky*.

The Spaniards anxiously dispatched the second-generation frontiersman, soldier, and explorer Don Juan Bautista de Anza to Monterey and San Francisco in 1774 and again in 1775, charging him to move the frontier as far north as possible from the little villages at Los Angeles and San Diego. In 1806 the Russians sent one of their most seasoned explorers to intersect with these Spanish advances. He was Nikolai Petrovich Rezanov, veteran of one voyage around the world, ambitious for preferment at court, and well acquainted with the benefits conferred upon Cortés by American adventures.

Rezanov was rebuffed, courteously but very firmly, by the Spanish governor, who was by that time installed at Monterey. But Rezanov got a sufficient glimpse of what lay inland to report to the czar that California might serve as the breadbasket of Kamchatka and Okhotsk. Russia was emerging as a great power; anything was possible. This was certainly true on the domestic front, for Rezanov became betrothed to Doña Concepción Arguello, daughter of the commandant at San Francisco. Though Rezanov found the governor "suspicious," the commandant was not. Unlike the Texas romance of the missions, this tale of early California ended in tragedy rather than ambiguity, for Rezanov died after being thrown from his horse as he was returning overland with his report.

By this time British naval forces had made regular appearances in what the Spaniards were calling the San Juan Islands, off Washington, and other Britons emerged on the shore of British Columbia after walking and paddling all the way across Canada to join the bickering.

Finally upstart Yankee skippers from New England joined hands with overlanders from St. Louis (yet another town named for the crusading king) following the path blazed by Lewis and Clark. The Oregon Trail gained traffic, and there was heard that faint drumbeat that would become the imperial war chant of the 1840s, "Fifty-four Forty or Fight!"

The missions of California were an answer as much to the British threat as to the Russians. We would all remember that if there had been a romance between some dashing Briton and yet another Spanish lady. There is, however, the melancholy tale of the Russian captain who fell in love with the daughter of the Spanish commander at San Francisco. Father Junipero Serra was in constant discussions with the military commanders who accompanied him to California. So far as I have been able to determine, he had no personal contact either with the Russians ashore or the British along the coast, but there is little doubt that they were present in his mind from the first reports of Cook's voyages until Serra's death in 1784.

There is a vast, contentious, and important literature about the effects of the Franciscans' mission activity upon the California Indians. No one disputes, however, that the subsequent loss of life and of culture was a tragedy, for the people affected, on a scale that matched the Great Dying of the sixteenth century. At least 80 percent of the California Indians died after they were gathered, sometimes forcibly, into compact communities where they built churches and raised crops under Spanish supervision and contracted diseases of Spanish introduction. Individual friars did all they could to mitigate the horrors of the system, dispensing medicine and kindness. By 1825 only shattered remnants remained of a diverse group of nations, including the opulent Chumash of the Santa Barbara coast.

Probably only the barely subsisting desert bands, who were never drawn into the Spanish system, were no worse off when the last mission was constructed in the Sonoma Valley than they had been when the Spaniards first appeared on the saint's day of San Diego in 1542.

LITERARY ARCHITECTURE: THE CASE OF RAMONA

Novelists have several times written scenarios for architecture. In 1807 William Beckford, author of the gothic thriller *Vathek*, completed a sham abbey at Fonthill in Wiltshire, England. Under its pseudo-cathedralic tower this most flamboyant of the heirs to American riches since the death of Cortés (Beckford inherited a fortune derived from West Indian sugar) began acting out his fantasies. Sadly, all doubts that the foundations of the ten-story tower were literary rather than lapidary were dispelled when it collapsed shortly thereafter.

Sir Walter Scott's Scottish baronial Abbotsford was a monument not only to the imaginary past of *Ivanhoe* but also to the insatiable appetite for such fables on the part of his contemporaries. Scott's tales of knights and damsels found places on a million parlor tables and were reanimated on opera stages from Buenos Aires to Cairo. Ivanhoe and Rebecca became more real to many people than Columbus or even Pocahontas. A hundred years later cinematic-literary architecture appeared when David Selznick's version of Tara was reproduced in a hundred suburban fantasies of *Gone with the Wind*.

Many of us received our first impressions of life in the California missions from Helen Hunt Jackson's *Ramona*, published in 1884, which sold more copies than any other novel written in America between *Uncle Tom's Cabin* and *Gone with the Wind*. The Mission Revival of the 1920s owes as much to *Ramona* as *both* the Scottish Baronial and the American Gothic Revival owe to *Ivanhoe* (though certainly Bertram Goodhue's impeccable instinct for pastiche helped the Mission Revival along). It is ironic that *Ramona* was not intended by its author to offer comfort in imaginary elysia. Instead Jackson intended it to be unsettling. She sought to use her novel as a weapon of social reform on behalf of the California Indians; she had tried history with *A Century of Dishonor* and social science with a detailed report to the Department of the Interior. Perhaps she could catch the conscience of the nation with a love story perfumed and embowered in prose such as this: "And the delicious, languid, semi-tropic summer came hovering over the valley. The apricots turned golden, the peaches glowed, the grapes filled and hardened, like opaque emeralds hung thick under the canopied vines. . . . There were lilies, and orange-blossoms, and poppies, and carnations, and geraniums in the pots, and musk — oh yes, ever and always musk.''

The musk overwhelmed the message. Reform was not in the air in bustling California, whose population grew from that of Kansas to that of Pennsylvania in Jackson's lifetime. Readers took from *Ramona* the sugar coating and left the nutrition behind. Instead of reform, California got revival — the Mission Revival. The Indians were forgotten and the friars romanticized. Everyone wanted whitewashed adobe with red-tiled roofs.

I have taken the musky quotation not directly from *Ramona* but from a wonderful description of its effects upon the archaeology and architecture of California by David Hurst Thomas, in the third volume of *Columbian Consequences* (1991). Anyone who is setting out upon a tour of the California missions should bring that essay along (perhaps a photocopy — the *Consequences* are weighty). Thomas has provided a consumer's guide to the authenticity of the missions, weighing their evidentiary value for students of California history. Those who have "restored" them have made such a study both necessary and possible; these buildings are *there*. Well, buildings like or partially like the originals are there. The missions might have decayed and disappeared into conditions intelligible only to archaeology or, more likely, into asphalt, making archaeology impossible. Parish life has continued under roofs repaired and walls stabilized by the enthusiasm unleashed by *Ramona*. On the other hand, the stage sets that have been created distract from, rather than enliven, the true drama of the past. Much evidence has been lost. Restoration is a dicey business.

From a religious point of view, some missions are extinct as places of worship, however pretty. Where they are still in use, and therefore alive, daily choices must be made between the imperatives of a worshiping community and the importunities of tourism. And there are other voices to be heard: another presence can be felt in nearly all these places, that of the Indians themselves. Under the altars and below the retablos of the Spaniards may be the holy places of the religions they replaced.

Many of the California missions are very beautiful as objects, but one should be wary of taking them as evidence of history. Some are painstaking simulations, in materials similar to those used originally; some are made of cement on steel frames; some are handsome representations of what the Franciscans might have built had they come into California at the height of the Mission Style of the 1920s or 1930s. All are worth visiting — warily.

Below: Fonts at San Juan Bautista, California. A thriving congregation, which includes many people of Indian descent, continues to worship in the freshly restored church. The mission has changed, perhaps for the better.

The following list owes much to David Thomas's research, though I have added interpretations of my own. This guide is offered in the hope that it may not engender the unintended consequences befalling *Ramona*.

At the end of the nineteenth century, only San Gabriel Arcángel (San Gabriel), San Buenaventura (Ventura), and Santa Bárbara among the large mission churches were still in use. Reasonably well preserved, they can be visited today and taken to be quite as they were when built. That statement must be modified in nearly all other cases.

San Francisco de Asís (in San Francisco on Dolores between 16th and 17th streets) was founded in 1776, and the present church was built between 1782 and 1791. It has been repaired but not "restored," a term often used to include "improvements." Its exterior, retablo, and many furnishings are still as Bret Harte described them in 1863, though cleaned and patched: "Its gouty pillars with plaster dropping away like tattered bandages, its rayless windows, its crumbling entrances, and the leper spots on its whitewashed wall eating through the dark adobe were relatively unchanged." Harte was not much interested in Muslim influences, but we should note that the retablo of San Francisco has a fine set of column capitals manifesting the medieval North African development of the Roman Corinthian form.

San Miguel Arcángel (halfway between Los Angeles and San Francisco, near Paso Robles off Highway 101 in an isolated setting) was founded in 1797 and is the least altered of all the California missions. The church was built between 1816 and 1818 and has miraculously retained its retablo and interior painting. It is the major surprise of the California missions. A very plain exterior contains an interior that is well worth a journey.

San Gabriel Arcángel (Mission Drive, San Gabriel) was founded in 1771; in 1834 it was secularized and its land holdings sold off. Construction of the church began in 1791; from 1859 to 1908 it was back in parish service before coming into the hands of the Claretian fathers. It suffered in the 1987 earthquake and is being carefully restored.

The first church at San Buenaventura (Main and Figueroa, Ventura) was built in 1782 and burned in 1791. A second church was consecrated in 1806, but both it and San Juan Capistrano were prostrated by an earthquake in 1812. San

Buenaventura, being small and simple, was more easily returned to use; after being secularized with the other missions it became a parish church in 1862. Thereafter it was Victorianized, but a *restoration* in 1959 brought it back to what earlier reports, old photographs, and drawings portrayed as its condition of the 1820s.

Santa Bárbara (Laguna Street, Santa Barbara), "Queen of Missions" did not have an unbroken reign, but she did better than all but San Francisco and San Miguel. Founded in 1786, the church was completed in accordance with a Spanish edition of Vitruvius in 1820. Though this mission, too, was secularized, it remained under the rule of the Franciscans, serving as a school, seminary, and hospice. Though the building is in remarkably good preservation, those who enjoy its flowery garden should be aware that no missions had such amenities. Santa Bárbara's garden was created after secularization.

San Juan Capistrano (on Interstate 5, San Juan Capistrano) is a splendid ruin, though its garden presents much too luxurious an impression of the windswept, gravelly earth of the actual mission compound. Father Junipero Serra's adobe church of the late 1770s was replaced by a six-domed masonry building nearly 150 feet high, largely the work of a Mexican stone mason from Culiacán, completed in 1806. It was shattered by the earthquake of 1812, secularized in the 1830s, restored and romanticized in the 1890s and 1920s. During one of these restorative sieges, a charge of gunpowder brought down still more of the fragile vaulting.

San Antonio de Padua (six miles north of Jolon) was founded in 1771, secularized, abandoned for forty-six years, partially restored in 1906, partially destroyed again by the earthquake of that year, and bulldozed down to the floor tiles in 1948 as part of a "conjectural restoration" that left only the original front facade and front colonnade. What one sees today, while charming, is a tribute not so much to the taste of the fathers as to that of William Randolph Hearst, who paid for a recreation in a style of which he approved.

San Carlos Borromeo de Carmelo (Carmel) is beautiful in a much grander way but is equally modern in its taste. After a succession of earlier churches (the first founded in 1770) had been destroyed and abondoned, a magnificent character named Henry Downie, baronet by inheritance and cabinetmaker by trade, determined to make a vision of

Ramona's California out of its crumbling, roofless walls. Wearing a Franciscan habit, Downie raised the money to raise the roof and restored as much of the original structure and as many of the furnishings as he could find. He created a new mission "the way they would have done it if they'd had a little money." One of his most inspired creations was the bowery garden, which, as Thomas informs us, "with its majestic fountain, was barren dirt during mission times."

As Winston Churchill said of the tales of King Arthur, if all this was not true, it should have been. The difficulty is that the heroism of friars and Indians alike is trivialized by the sweet, theatrical luxury of such places. Thomas reproduces a photograph of the pile of dusty rubble which as late as 1920 covered the site of Father Serra's cell, now a favorite tourist attraction at Carmel. Though a tiny sign acknowledges that the room is a "reconstruction," the prevailing impression surely must be that Downie's creation actually was occupied by Serra.

For me, the most satisfying of all the California churches associated with the missions is the Asistencia de San Antonio de Pala (Pala, nineteen miles northeast of San Luis Rey), a tiny reconstructed church based on a portion of its walls remaining after an earthquake. Still in regular parish use by the local Indians of the Pala Reservation, the church lies behind a frequently swept gravel plaza. The clergy are still doing what their predecessors did in 1815, and so is the building. The columns running down the center of the church are an accurate statement of the means by which the original builders bridged a wide span with not-so-wide timbers. Bernard Fontana informs us that this is what the Jesuits did at San Xavier in the 1750s and 1760s.

La Purísima Concepción at Lompoc.

History has fallen out in such a way that one receives the best sense of what the larger missions were actually like from the total reconstruction from the ground up of La Purísima Concepción (twenty miles by road northwest of Buellton), founded in 1787. It lies beside an intermittent stream four miles northeast of Lompoc below a red-sand California hillside covered with trees that survive with little water. Earthquakes, Indian uprisings, and secularization brought the mission low, but in the 1930s the state of California, the National Park Service, the Civilian Conservation Corps, and Santa Barbara County undertook a complete archaeological survey, which led to a meticulous — and very moving — reconstruction of eighteen buildings, corrals, and pools, and even of some farming of the sort that might have been carried on at the mission.

The next four churches are not surviving examples of the Spanish missions. That does not mean that they are not worth a journey in the Michelin sense. Nor does it decry the skill by which the appearance of lost examples may have been recreated. But visitors should be aware that they are entirely simulated, with greater or lesser relationship to either documentary or archaeological evidence of the "originals."

San Francisco Solano (Sonoma, on State Highway 12) was founded in 1823. The church of 1824 was lost. The present church is a building that was remodeled in 1841 and heavily restored from 1911 to 1913. It is now a museum.

San José de Guadalupe (Fremont, State Highway 21) was founded and the first church completed in 1797. It was replaced in 1809 and destroyed by earthquake in 1868. The present structure was built in the 1980s.

Santa Cruz (Emmet and School streets, Santa Cruz) was founded in 1791; the church was completed in 1794 and destroyed in 1857. The present church was built in 1889. A "replica" of the mission church was built nearby in 1931.

San Fernando Rey de España (15151 San Fernando Mission Boulevard, Mission Hills) was founded in 1797. A church was completed in 1799, but San Fernando quickly became more a hostelry than a mission, for it was on a major highway. The present church, built of lath and plaster after the earthquake of 1971, is explicitly stated to be (except in its materials) a replica.

San Luis Rey de Francia (San Luis Rey, off State Highway 76) was founded in 1797 or 1798 (authorities differ). The present church was completed in 1815 and abandoned in 1865. Reconstruction, based upon some portion of the original, was begun before 1900. It is now a Franciscan college.

San Diego de Alcalá (five miles east of State Highway 5, off State Highway 8, on the outskirts of San Diego) was founded in 1769. The church was rebuilt between 1808 and 1813 and abandoned in 1835. The new church was built in 1931, behind a facade that is probably authentic.

San Antonio de Padua (23 miles southwest of King City, on a military reservation but open to the public) was founded in 1771. The church was completed in 1813 and abandoned in 1882. A new church was put back into liturgical use in 1949 behind a restoration of the original facade.

Santa Inés (Solvang) was founded in 1804. The church was constructed between 1813 and 1817 and is now restored with its small convento.

The church at San Juan Bautista was founded in 1797. The present structure was completed in 1812 and heavily restored between 1949 and 1950.

Nuestra Señora de la Soledad (three miles south of Soledad) was founded and the first church completed in 1791. It collapsed in 1831; a replacement chapel was built in 1832 and restored in 1954.

San Luis Obispo de Tolosa (in San Luis Obispo) was founded in 1772, burned three times, and abandoned in the 1830s. It was reconstructed in the 1870s as a New England church, gutted by fire in the 1920s, restored and returned to parish use after 1934.

Left: The arched colonnades at San Luis Rey de Francia.

Opposite: San Francisco de Asís, in San Francisco, was founded in 1776, and the present church built between 1782 and 1791. The facade is much restored.

The nave and retablo of San Francisco de Asis.

The pulpit at St. Miguel Arcángel, San Miguel, California. The preaching ministry flourished on the mission frontier, responding to Protestantism with a Counter Reformation emphasis upon scripture and the word.

With the simplest of means, the friars and Indians at San Miguel Arcángel effected a synthesis of Arabic, Spanish, and American ornament.

The altar of San Miguel.

Above: San Buenaventura in Ventura.

Opposite: A painted arch at San Miguel.

Overleaf: The symbolism of Old World continuities on the exterior of the mission at Ventura: columns, swags, and a North African doorway.

Above: Ornament from very old European folk traditions cheerfully survives in the mission church of San Buenaventura.

Opposite: Vitruvius comes to California: the facade of the mission of Santa Bárbara, founded in 1786 and completed in 1820.

186

The interior of the cloister at Santa Bárbara is magnificently maintained. It is too gorgeous to represent actual mission conditions.

Above: San Juan Capistrano, California. A modern painted arch is in the old tradition of Spain, which reaches back to Roman ornament. A bit of Pompeii in another earthquake belt.

Opposite: The chapel of Father Serra at San Juan Capistrano remains as part of a complex of magnificent multidomed ruins. The late Franciscan grandeur of the main church lasted only six years.

Above: San Juan Bautista.

Below: San José de Guadalupe, Fremont.

Above: San Luis Obispo de Tolosa.

Below: San Francisco Solano, Sonoma.

San Antonio de Padua, California, was founded in 1771, and the church completed in 1813. The church was rebuilt to its full Franciscan length with a hint of gothicity in 1949 behind a restored but largely original facade.

Opposite: The confessional at San Antonio de Padua.

Opposite and above: San Antonio de Padua, California, twice destroyed by earthquakes, was reconstructed imaginatively by William Randolph Hearst. Throughout, the spirit remained and may still be felt in this place off the main tourist routes.

Above and opposite: San Carlos Borromeo de Carmelo is a tribute in equal measure to the Franciscans of the 1770s and to its reconstructive genius, Henry Downie, after the 1930s.

Opposite: Rich textures on a wall in Carmel.

San Diego de Alcalá, California, founded in 1769, was rebuilt behind the probably authentic facade of 1813 in 1931.

The bell tower of the Asistencia de San Antonio de Pala, California.

Pala, a true mission church, still serves the Indians on a small reservation.

202

A simple colonnade at the Asistencia de San Antonio de Pala.
The church was built in 1815, destroyed by earthquake, and
rebuilt.

The interior of the reconstructed mission at Lompoc is closer to the original than most restorations.

The reconstruction gives a sense of the starkness of its cloister.

Above: A reconstructed dormitory for young Indian girls at La Purísima Concepción at Lompoc. Purity, perhaps, but not much freedom.

Opposite: Vitruvius moves inside: the exterior of Santa Bárbara is echoed in the design of the organ at San José de Guadalupe in Fremont. The present church, containing this loft, was built in 1982–1985.

Above: The original font at San José de Guadalupe.   *Opposite:* The altar and retablo.

Above, right, and opposite:
San Luis Rey de Francia was founded in 1797/98.
Reconstruction was begun about 1900.
The patron saint of San Luis Rey de Francia was Louis IX of
France, whose name was also given to St. Louis, Missouri.

Freshly painted and newly recreated, San Francisco Solano
suggests what many of the smaller mission sanctuaries may have
looked like when they were new.

Overleaf and below: The interior of San Juan Bautista, altered into an uncanonical three-aisled form that serves an active congregation very well. Handsomely reornamented in the old tradition.

Opposite: The bell tower at San Juan Bautista.

San Luis Opispo de Tolosa was founded in 1772, burned and abandoned, reconstructed in the 1870s as a New England church, burned and gutted in the 1920s, restored to a Spanish style, and returned to parish use after 1934.

Overleaf and below: San Luis Obispo.

SUMMING UP

THE VISIBLE ACCOMPLISHMENT of the missions is in the remaining buildings throughout Mexico and in that common province that is the Mexican Northwest and the American Southwest. There seems to be a church or the ruin of a church everywhere a friar might hope for a few converts. Some of these ruins, such as those at Quarai, Abo, and Gran Quivira (in the group southeast of Albuquerque) and San Juan Capistrano in California, magnificently memorialize not failure, I believe, but the *completion* of an endeavor. That endeavor brought disease and death and the destruction of ancient cultures having qualities as admirable as those of medieval Europe. It disrupted religious practices as subtle and, one may assume, as efficacious as those it brought, in the eyes of a tolerant God. Still, at its best, at the highest of its aspirations, it was as noble as any other endeavor in human history, certainly as noble as the Crusades, of which it was the westward extension.

Perhaps the mission effort was a surge of medievalism attempted too late. Perhaps it should be understood, as some suggest, as the garrisoning of colonial outposts with a militant priesthood. Perhaps its churches should be equated with the temples of Mithra along Hadrian's Wall marking the northernmost frontier of Rome, or with Rome's other temples in Dacia or Syria.

But I do not believe this tale to be so flat and simple. Europe came forth in all its confusions and passions and spent its energies seeking empire in the Americas. It was prepared to kill to become rich, to enslave in order to become powerful. Europe also brought death it did not intend through the insidious invasion of its own diseases and those of the Africans it forced to do its will.

But Europe also had gifts to bestow. There is no way to persuade anyone of the value of those gifts of faith if he or she does not think them so. One might allege, as some have, that the friars were engaged in a pernicious undertaking. They did not see it that way. If motivation matters — and it does — the worst one can say of them is that however misguided, many of them were, in medieval terms, "holy fools."

I do not think there is, on this side of the frontier between the tangible and the intangible, a confident assessment to be made of the mission. Its spiritual achievement and its spiritual cost can be weighed only in scales beyond that frontier. And so, as we often do in history, we come back to the beginning.

THE SPREAD OF MISSIONS

The Missions of Spanish North America Discussed in This Book

SONOMA

SAN FRANCISCO

CALIFORNIA

LOS ANGELES

SAN DIEGO

PHOENIX

ARIZONA

TUCSON

Apache

SONORA

ALBUQUERQUE

SANTA FE

NEW MEXICO

Comanche

EL PASO

Rio Grande

TEXAS

BAJA

SOUTH CAROLINA

GEORGIA

JACKSONVILLE

ST. AUGUSTINE

MOBILE

TALLAHASSEE

FLORIDA

SAN ANTONIO

MIAMI

LA
IGLESIA
DE
SAN ISIDRO

Overleaf: A small church near Taos Mountain at the northeastern limit of the missions of the Rio Grande.

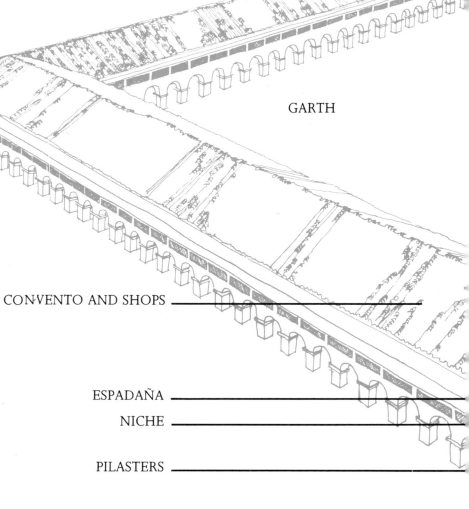

GARTH

CONVENTO AND SHOPS

ESPADAÑA

NICHE

PILASTERS

OCULUS

MAIN PORTAL

NICHE

An interior niche, Cristo Rey, Santa Fe.

A MISSION FROM ABOVE

SAN LUIS REY DE FRANCIA, CALIFORNIA

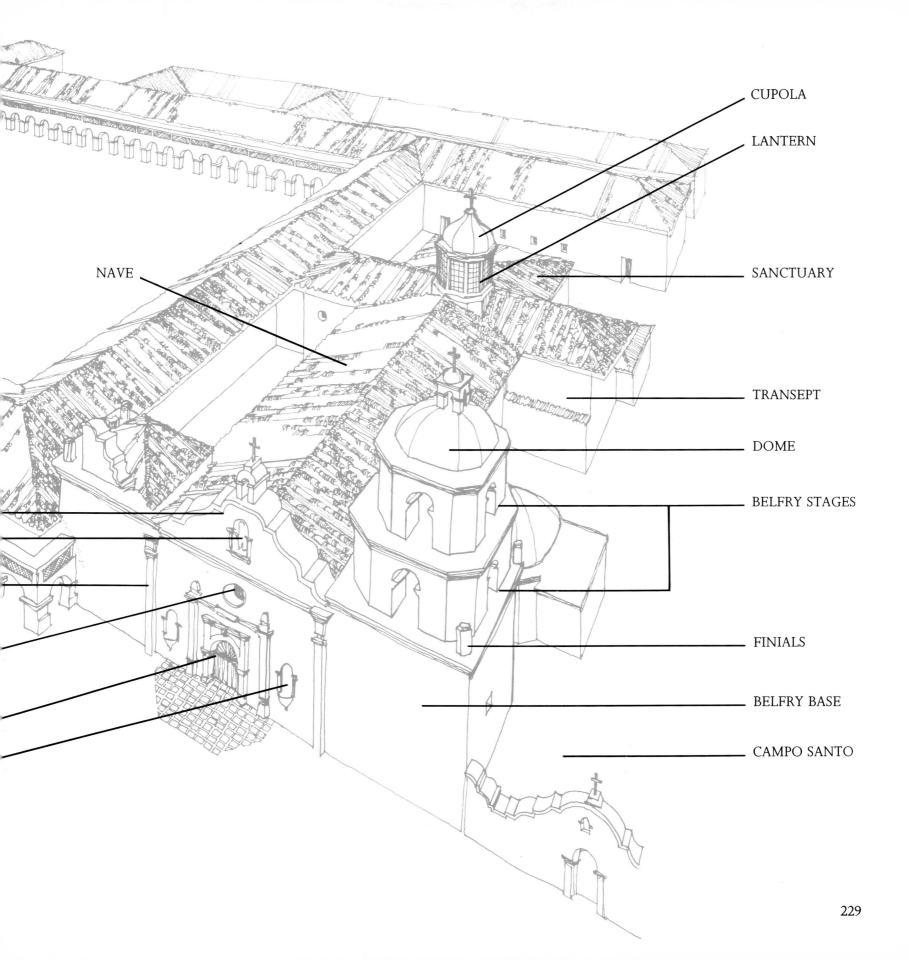

CUPOLA

LANTERN

NAVE

SANCTUARY

TRANSEPT

DOME

BELFRY STAGES

FINIALS

BELFRY BASE

CAMPO SANTO

229

THE APSE OF A MISSION CHURCH

SAN XAVIER DEL BAC, ARIZONA

DOME

DRUM

SQUINCH

ARCH

SANTO BULTO

RETABLO MAYOR

SANCTUARY

TABERNACLE

ALTAR

ALTAR RAILING

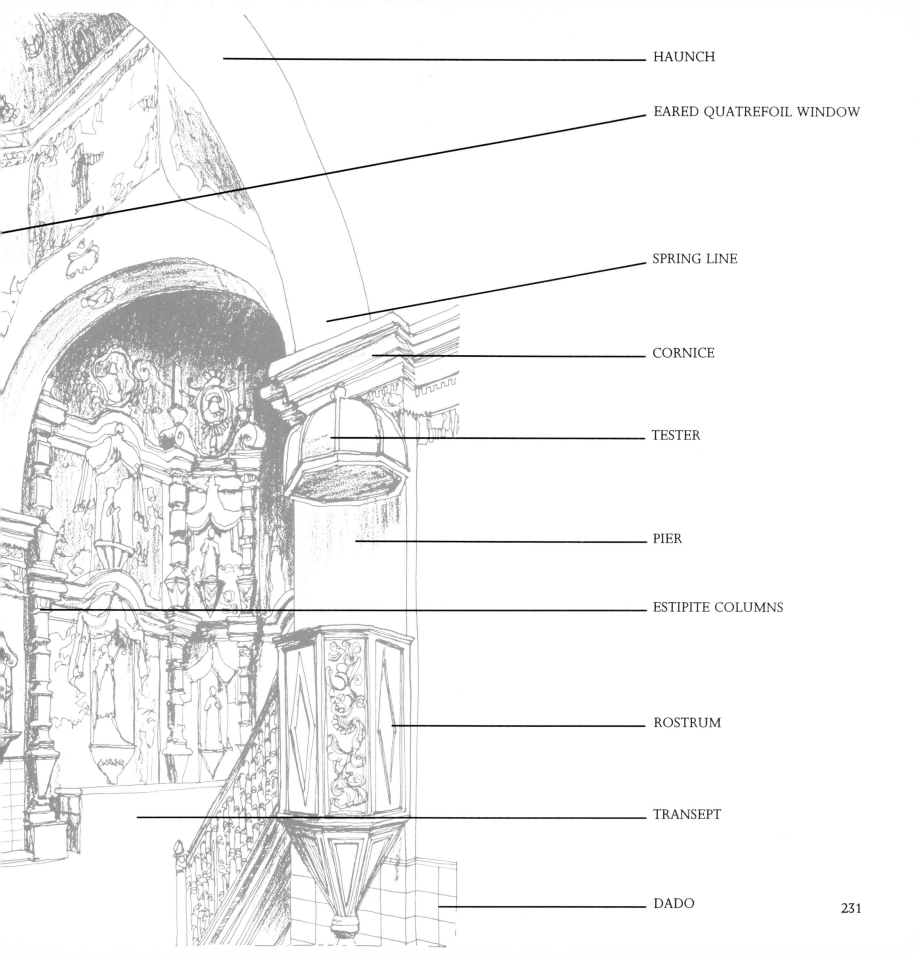

HAUNCH

EARED QUATREFOIL WINDOW

SPRING LINE

CORNICE

TESTER

PIER

ESTIPITE COLUMNS

ROSTRUM

TRANSEPT

DADO

231

GLOSSARY

The following terms are used in connection with the mission, its art, furnishings, architecture, and personnel. Architectural elements that can be seen easily in the illustrations will be found there rather than described below.

ADOBE
Sun-dried (rather than fired) mud bricks. Straw or ash may be used to bind the mud.

APSE
The termination of the main aisle or nave of a church, containing the main altar and main altarpiece (*retablo mayor*). It is usually located at the end of the church opposite the main door.

ALTAR
That upon which a sacrifice is offered. It may be a table upon which Mass is offered, or a consecrated altar stone supported by a table.

ASISTENCIA
A sub-mission, comparable to a *visita*.

ATRIUM
An open area or court in front of a church, usually delimited by a low wall.

BULTO
A sculptured religious image.

CABECERA
The principal church in a mission district. The priest lived here and serviced the smaller churches or chapels from this base. Also see *visita* and *asistencia*.

CAMPO SANTO
Cemetery.

CANALES
Rainwater spouts on a roof.

COLEGIO
A college, a training school for missionaries.

CONVENTO
In the missions the word applies to the working quarters, housing, and living complexes for the regular clergy.

CORBEL
An architectural element, either wood or stone, protruding from a wall and used to support beams, rafters and, occasionally, arches.

DESAGÜE (OR DESAGUADERO)
Drainage channels down sides of walls.

FRIAR
A member of a mendicant order: Dominican, Franciscan, Carmelite, or Augustinian.

GARTH
An open courtyard, usually part of the cloister. Also called a *patio*.

GENTE DE RAZÓN
Literally "people of reason," this is a term used generally to designate non-Indians or Indians that had become assimilated. There is the further implication that they were Christians.

NAVE
The central aisle of the church and the portion of the church that holds the congregation.

NICHE
A recessed area in a wall or *retablo* to hold and present a religious image or article.

PLAZA
An open area, usually in the center of a settlement, around which are arranged governmental and religious buildings forming a square or rectangle.

PORTAL
Any entrance to a building.

PORTERÍA
A porter's lodge, a reception area, and one of the two entrances to the *convento*.

232

REFECTORY
The dining hall in a *convento*.

RETABLO
An altar screen. The elaborate architectural support for paintings and/or religious sculpture found behind an altar against a wall. Every colonial baroque Mexican church had at least one. Also called retable, reredo, or altarpiece.

SACRISTY
A room usually attached to the church with direct access to the sanctuary. Vestments, books, and sacred vessels were kept here, and priests prepared and robed for services in this room.

SANCTUARY
The part of the church reserved for the clergy, separated from the congregation by a low railing. The most sacred part of the church, containing the main altar.

SALA DE PROFUNDIS
A room in the *convento* where the clerical community could meet or meditate — similar to a small chapel.

SANTO
Literally "saint," "saintly," or "holy." A common term for religious imagery, either two- or three-dimensional.

SOTOCORO
A vestibule or area under the choir loft.

TABERNACLE
A cupboard-like case attached to the altar which held the consecrated host and wine of the Blessed Sacrament. The interior of the tabernacle is lined or decorated, and the door's interior and exterior are usually covered with symbols and decorations.

VISITA
A village or chapel that was visited by a priest from the *cabecera*. There could be more than one *visita* for each *cabecera*.

Above: Interior of Santo Angel, Satevo; the paintings, of which only remnants remain, were possibly made by the architect, Father Luis Martin, before 1767.

APPENDIX
SOME REDISCOVERED ARCHITECTS AND ARTISANS

At San Antonio de Valero in San Antonio, Texas, two French architects, "Francisco el Frances" and Juan de Medaville, were at work in 1718 and 1719. Antonio de Tello, described as Spanish but possibly Italian, was there in 1741 as a master mason. In the 1750s an unnamed Indian master mason from Aguascalientes was "master of the church project." He was succeeded in the late 1760s by an Indian master mason named Estevan de Losoya or de el Oio.

The redoubtable historian Mardith Schuetz, who has ferreted out the names of these long-unrecognized Texas artisans, suggests that another Indian, of the Tilpacopal nation, named Nicolas, should be credited with the baptismal font and other sculpture at Nuestra Señora de la Purísima Concepción in San Antonio. She also has discovered the trail of Antonio Salazar, an Indian master mason from Zacatecas, who worked at San José y San Miguel de Aguayo from the 1760s until the 1790s, bringing there the peculiar ornament that might be called Zacatecesque. Pedro (sometimes called Juan) Huizar, a mulatto, is famous among mission lovers for his remarkable sculpture at San José. He, too, came to San Antonio from Aguascalientes, some twenty years after his anonymous colleague at San Antonio de Valero.

The decorative schemes of San Antonio de Valero in Texas and that of San Xavier del Bac in Arizona may well have been based upon a single format given to the Franciscan builders of each church. The scheme was triangular, placing Saints Claire and Margaret in attendance on the Virgin Mary.

James Ivey of the National Park Service has generously contributed the following summary of many years of his own research into the identity of other artisans and architects of the missions of the American Southwest:

> Fray Bautista Velderrain directed the construction of San Xavier del Bac from about 1783 to 1797; we don't yet know the name of the mason(s) who designed and built the building. Before Bac, Fray Velderrain was at Suaqui [Sonora], where he oversaw the construction of San Ignacio. The designer of the original plan of [San Antonio de] Valero, on the other hand, was Maestro Antonio de Tello, about 1738. The Franciscans apparently finished Valero with a flat roof and some sort of simple bell tower in the late 1740s after Tello fled town; the building collapsed after November of 1749 and before mid-1751. It was rebuilt about 1751 under the direction of Maestro Hieronymo Ybarra from San Luis Potosí, apparently following a modernized version of Tello's original plans and building on the first three or four feet of Tello's construction. Ybarra (and the master sculptor Felipe de Santiago, who was hired with him) was apparently fired or quit in late 1759 before he could finish the Valero church; it was probably worked on by Maestro Nicholas Albanil, from Mission Concepción, for one or two years after 1760. Then Maestro Estevan de Losoya was brought to town, but he died in 1767. Maestro Dionicio Gonzales was hired to finish the job in the same year but was apparently pulled off the project in 1772, just as the ribs were being finished and the vaulting started, to complete San José.

NOTES

24   The church at Trampas, New Mexico: I am indebted to Bernard Fontana for the information that transverse clerestories were in place at La Purísima de Socorro in Texas, and in New Mexico churches at Socorro, Santa Cruz, Santa Ana, and Isleta as well as at Trampas. He informs me that a much grander example of the form is in the sixteenth-century Nuestra Señora de Guadalupe church at Juarez in Chihuahua.

24   The Pimería Alta: "Arizona" is an invention of 1863, when it was carved out of the territory of New Mexico and given a name. New Mexico had been carved out of the broader region that was called Pimería Alta until the treaties after the Mexican War drove an international border across the region, artificially dividing its mission field.

24   The two orders favored different materials: Bernard Fontana adds that there were a few exceptions to this rule. The early Franciscans used the sun-dried material in Arizona at Tumacácori and its visita at Calabasas and, in the nineteenth century, at a third, Santa Ana del Cuiquiburito.

29   "The Shield of Saint Patrick": I have used the translation and arrangement of N. D. O'Donoghue, from James P. Mackey, ed., *An Introduction to Celtic Christianity* (Edinburgh: T. & T. Clark, 1989), p. 47.

31   Description of the Texas Indians: Kathleen Gilmore, "The Indians of Mission Rosario," in *Columbian Consequences*, vol. 1, ed. David Hurst Thomas (Washington: Smithsonian Institution, 1989), pp. 232, 236.

31   "Both the tallest and the shortest . . .": Julia G. Costello and David Hornbeck, "Alta California: An Overview," in *Columbian Consequences*, vol. 1, p. 305.

31 Studies correlating dispersion of languages and dispersion of animals and plants: I have had to simplify considerably the monographs I have found on the subject of glottochronology by its proponents and adverse critics, and as usual to bring together what can be found in general texts with specialized material coming to hand. I am grateful to Robert S. Hoffman for lending me a paper he is working on with Richard A. Rogers, L. A. Rogers, and Larry D. Martin, entitled "Native American Biological Diversity and Ice Age Refugia." I have also consulted Richard Rogers, Larry Martin, and T. Dale Nicklas, "Ice-Age Geography and the Distribution of Native North American Languages," *Journal of Biogeography* 17 (1990), 131–43.

36 The Jewish strain in Spanish life: See Jaime Vicens Vives, *An Economic History of Spain* (Princeton: Princeton University Press, 1969).

38 On Christian and Muslim intermarriage and Jewish leadership in Muslim Spain, I have summarized what I have learned from John H. Crow, *Spain, the Root and the Flower* (Berkeley: University of California Press, 1985), pp. 61–62.

39 Vargas Llosa: "Questions of Conquest," *Harper's Magazine*, December 1990, pp. 45 ff.

49 Father Kino: Jorge Olvera, in *Dove of the Desert* (no. 4., Winter 1989), the newsletter of the Friends of San Xavier Mission, points out that Kino spent two years in the portion of Spain most deeply influenced by Muslim culture and that his ground plans resemble Lower Andalusian mosques remodeled into Christian churches.

54 The word "troubador": I am indebted to Jonathan Bloom of Richmond, New Hampshire, one of the world's experts on Islamic architecture, for the origins of both "troubador" and "lute," along with some very kind assistance in keeping me from making mistakes in this highly specialized field. Those mistakes remaining are my own.

75 Norman Neuerburg: Neuerburg's fine book, *The Decoration of the California Missions* (Santa Barbara, Calif.: Bellerophon Books, 1989), shows how the Santa Clara mission would appear with its full panoply of color restored. The book is worth buying for the cover alone.

76 "The richest ornament . . .": Kurt Baer, *Architecture of the California Missions* (Berkeley: University of California Press, 1958), p. 63.

76 The "striking star window": *The California Missions*, edited by the staff of Sunset Books (Menlo Park, Calif.: Lane Book Co., 1968), p. 63. I am not absolutely certain that the writers were making a joke. The best evidence that they were is the publication in the same book of a similarly shaped star fountain at San Gabriel (p. 110) and another star window at San Rafael (p. 299).

86 Round, domed *mysteria*: Those of us who came to the study of architecture out of a shock of admiration for the dazzling apparitions provided by Louis Sullivan to small towns such as Owatonna, Minnesota, and Sidney, Ohio, and to cemeteries in St. Louis and Chicago, have found additional delight in following his curiosity into Muslim funerary buildings. Sullivan's Getty, Ryerson, and Wainwright tombs can be fully apprehended only when they are seen as the terminal glories of a sequence that began in the sanctuaries of mystery cults and the tombs of Syrian heroes, proceeded across North Africa in multitudes of prototypes, especially in places such as Qayrawan in Tunisia, and reappeared in this hemisphere in such structures as the tile chapel in the monastery of San Diego in the town of Cherubusco in the Federal District of Mexico.

90 The church at Satevo: Richard Fisher's booklets on the backcountry of northwestern Mexico and the Sea of Cortés are among the most colorful sources available for nonspecialists. See his *National Parks of Mexico* (Tucson, Ariz.: Sunracer Publications, 1990). In March 1991 Bernard Fontana, in the newsletter of the Southwestern Mission Research Center, printed an extensive report on the church at Satevo, demonstrating that it was built between 1739 and 1767 (the year of the Jesuits' expulsion) and adding some crucial details as to its governance.

90 The judgment hall of the king of Parthia: This description, and much else in these paragraphs, is drawn from E. Baldwin Smith, *The Dome* (Princeton, N.J.: Princeton University Press, 1971), p. 82.

96 "None of the imposing Spanish colonial churches . . .": Charles W. Polzer, *Kino Guide II* (Tucson, Ariz.: Southwestern Mission Research Center), p. 39.

96 Henry A. Crabb: I am grateful to Bernard Fontana for correcting my misconception of this siege.

104 The definitive discussion of these subjects: Gutierrez's masterly work, which covers the entire terrain of "marriage, sexuality, and power in New Mexico, 1500–1846," is entitled *When Jesus Came, the Corn Mothers Went Away* (Palo Alto, Calif.: Stanford University Press, 1991).

104 "From the Pueblos south . . .": Gutierrez, *When Jesus Came*, pp. 29–30.

108 They operated under royal charters: Eugene Lyon, in a wonderful essay, "The Enterprize of Florida," in *Columbian Consequences*, vol. 2, p. 283.

108 "Your own land . . .": The king to Ayllon, quoted in Lyon, "The Enterprize," p. 285.

111 Indian murals: The quotations are from Gary Shapiro and John H. Hann, "The Documentary Image of the Council Houses," in *Columbian Consequences*, vol. 3, pp. 512–13.

112 "Periodic food shortages . . .": Summary of findings by Larsen, Shoeninger, Hutchinson, Russell, and Ruff, "Beyond Demographic Collapse," in *Columbian Consequences*, vol. 3, p. 423.

115 "Kino churches": Bernard Fontana points out that along with the surviving Jesuit ruins and the portions of their work incorporated into Franciscan missions, the church at Oquitoa, in Sonora, is probably Jesuit with a Franciscan facade.

118 Father Bernard Middendorff: Bernard Fontana informs me that Middendorff was the only resident priest in Tucson during the Hispanic period. He was forced out of the little town after one year, and no other priest was assigned until 1866.

BIBLIOGRAPHY

Adams, and Chavez. *The Missions of New Mexico, 1776*. Albuquerque, N.M.: University of New Mexico Press, 1973.

Ahlborn, Richard. *The San Antonio Missions: Edward Everett and the American Occupation, 1847*. Fort Worth, Tex.: Amon Carter Museum, 1985.

Almaraz, Felix. *The San Antonio Missions and Their System of Land Tenure*. Austin, Tex.: University of Texas Press, 1989.

Archibald, Richard. *Economic Aspects of the California Missions*. Washington: Academy of American Franciscan History, 1978.

Baer, Kurt. *Architecture of the California Missions*. Berkeley: University of California Press, 1958.

Bannon, John. *The Spanish Borderland Frontier 1513–1821*. Albuquerque, N.M.: University of New Mexico Press, 1974.

Bezy, John, and Joseph Sanchez, eds. *Pecos: Gateway to the Pueblos and the Plains*. Tucson, Ariz.: Southwest Park and Monuments Association, 1988.

Bezy, John V., and Joseph P. Sanchez. *Pecos: Gateway to Pueblos and Plains*. Tucson, Ariz.: Southwest Parks and Monuments Association, 1988.

Bleser, Nicholas J. *Tumacácori: From Rancheria to National Monument*. Tucson, Ariz.: Southwest Parks and Monuments Association, 1990.

Bottineau, Yves. *Iberian-American Baroque*. New York: Grosset and Dunlap, 1970.

Briggs, Walter. *Without the Noise of Arms: The 1776 Dominguez-Escalante Search*. Flagstaff, Ariz.: Northland Press, 1976.

Brooks, Charles, M., Jr. *Texas Missions: Their Romance and Architecture*. Dallas: Dealy and Lowe, 1936.

The California Missions, ed. Sunset Books. Menlo Park, Calif.: Lane Book Company, 1964.

The California Missions: The Earliest Series of Views Made in 1856. Santa Barbara, Calif.: Bellerophon Books, 1988.

Conant, John. *The Pelican History of Art: Carolingian and Romanesque Architecture, 800–1200*. New York: Penguin Books, 1959.

Crow, John H. *Spain: The Root and the Flower*. Berkeley: University of California Press, 1985.

Cruz, Gilberto Rafael. *Let There Be Towns: Spanish Municipal Origins in the American Southwest, 1610–1810*. College Station, Tex.: Texas A&M University Press, 1988.

Donahue, John A. *After Kino: Jesuit Missions in Northwestern New Spain, 1711–1767*, Sources and Studies for the History of the Americas, vol. 6. St. Louis: Jesuit Historical Institute, 1969.

Elliot, J. H. *Imperial Spain 1469–1716*. New York: St. Martin's Press, 1964.

Engelhardt, Zephyrin. *The Missions and Missionaries of California*. Santa Barbara, Calif.: Mission Santa Barbara, 1930.

Fontana, Bernard L. *Entrada: The Legacy of Spain and Mexico in the United States*. Tucson, Ariz.: Southwest Parks and Monuments Association, forthcoming.

Foster, George. *Culture and Conquest: America's Spanish Heritage*. New York: Werner-Gren Foundation for Anthropological Research, 1960.

Garrigues, Emilio. *The Oneness of the Americas: Conquistadores at Trial*. Madrid: Ediciones Cultura, 1969.

Geiger, Maynard. *Franciscan Missions in Hispanic California*. San Marino, Calif.: Huntington Library, 1969.

Goodwin, Godfrey. *Islamic Spain*. San Francisco: Chronicle Books, 1990.

Gutierrez, Ramon. "The Death of Padre Jesus and Mother Maria: The 1680 Pueblo Revolt Reconsidered." Unpublished paper.

———. *When Jesus Came, the Corn Mothers Went Away: Marriage, Sexuality and Power in New Mexico 1500–1846*. Palo Alto, Calif.: Stanford University Press, 1991.

Hayes, Alden. *The Four Churches at Pecos*. Albuquerque, N.M.: University of New Mexico Press, 1974.

Hudson, Charles. *The Juan Pardo Expeditions: Explorations of the Carolinas and Tennessee, 1566–1568*. Washington: Smithsonian Institution Press, 1990.

Hutt, Anthony. *Islamic Architecture, North Africa*. London: Scorpion, 1977.

Ivey, James. *In the Midst of Loneliness: The Architectural History of the Salinas Missions*, professional paper no. 15. Santa Fe, N.M.: Southwest Cultural Resources Center, 1990.

Kellermen, Pal. *Medieval American Art*. New York: Macmillan, 1943.

Kessett, John. *Kiva, Cross and Crown: The Pecos Indians and New Mexico, 1540–1840*. Albuquerque, N.M.: University of New Mexico Press, 1987.

Kessell, John L. *The Missions of New Mexico Since 1776*. Albuquerque, N.M.: University of New Mexico Press, 1980.

Kubler, George, and Martin Soria. *Art and Architecture in Spain and Portugal and their American Dominions 1500–1800*. Baltimore: Penguin Books, 1959.

———. *The Religious Architecture of New Mexico in the Colonial Period and since the American Occupation*. Colorado Springs, Colo.: Taylor Museum, 1940.

Limerick, Patricia N. *The Legacy of Conquest: The Unbroken Past of the American West*. New York: Norton, 1987.

Liss, Peggy. *Mexico Under Spain 1521–1556*. Chicago: University of Chicago Press, 1975.

Mackay, A. *Spain in the Middle Ages: From Frontier to Empire*. New York: Macmillan, 1977.

Mackey, James P. *An Introduction to Celtic Christianity*. Edinburgh: T. & T. Clark, 1989.

McNeill, William. "The Gunpowder Revolution." *Quarterly Journal of Military History* 3 (1), August 1990.

Milanich, Jerald, and Susan Milbrath, eds. *First Encounters: Spanish Explorations in the Caribbean and the United States, 1492–1570*. Gainesville, Fla.: University of Florida Press, 1989.

Montgomery, Ross, Watson Smith, and John Brew. *Franciscan Awatovi: The Excavation and Conjectural Reconstruction of a 17th-Century Spanish Mission*. Papers of the Peabody Museum, vol. 36, report no. 3. Cambridge, Mass.: Peabody Museum, 1949.

Murphy, Dan. *Salinas Pueblo Missions: Abó, Quarai, and Gran Quivira*. Tucson, Ariz.: Southwest Parks and Monuments Association, 1993.

Nabokov, Peter. *Indian Running: Native American History and Tradition*. Santa Fe, N.M.: Ancient City Press, 1981.

Neuerburg, Norman. *The Decoration of the California Missions*. Santa Barbara, Calif.: Bellerophon Books, 1989.

Officer, James. *Hispanic America 1536–1856*. Tucson, Ariz.: University of Arizona Press, 1987.

Parry, J. H. *The Spanish Seaboard Empire*. Berkeley: University of California Press, 1966.

Peterson, Kenneth. *Climate and the Dolores River Anasazi*. University of Utah Archaeological Papers no. 113. Salt Lake City, Utah, 1988.

Polzer, Charles. *Kino Guide II: His Missions — His Monuments*. Tucson, Ariz.: Southwest Mission Research Center, 1982.

Porter, Eliot, and Ellan Auerbach. *Mexican Churches*. Albuquerque, N.M.: University of New Mexico Press, 1987.

Pratt, Boyd. "The Plaza in History." *El Palacio* 94 (2), Winter 1988.

Richardson, William. *Mexico Through Russian Eyes, 1806–1940*. Pittsburgh, Pa.: University of Pittsburgh Press, 1988.

Roca, Paul. *Spanish Jesuit Churches in Mexico's Tarahumara*. Tucson, Ariz.: University of Arizona Press, 1979.

Sanford, Trent. *The Story of Architecture in Mexico*. New York: Norton, 1947.

Smith, E. Baldwin. *The Dome*. Princeton: Princeton University Press, 1971.

Spicer, Edward. *Cycles of Conquest: The Impact of Spain, Mexico and the United States on the Indians of the Southwest, 1533–1960*. Tucson, Ariz.: University of Arizona Press, 1962.

Swanton, John, ed. *Final Report of the United States De Soto Expedition Commission*. Washington: Smithsonian Institution Press, 1985.

Sweet, Jill. *Dances of the Tewa Pueblo Indians*. Santa Fe, N.M.: School of American Research Press, 1985.

Thomas, David, ed. *Columbian Consequences*. Washington: Smithsonian Institution Press, 1990.

Torres, Luis. *San Antonio Missions National Historical Park*. Tucson, Ariz.: Southwest Parks and Monuments Association, 1993.

Vicens Vives, Jaime. *An Economic History of Spain*. Princeton: Princeton University Press, 1969.

Webber, David. *The Mexican Frontier 1821–1846: The American Southwest under Mexico*. Albuquerque, N.M.: University of New Mexico Press, 1982.

Weddle, Robert. *San Juan Bautista: Gateway to Spanish Texas*. Austin, Tex.: University of Texas Press, 1968.

Weiss, Elizabeth. *Art and Time in Mexico*. New York: Harper and Row, 1985.

Wills, W. H. *Early Prehistoric Agriculture in the American Southwest*. Santa Fe, N.M.: School of American Research Press, 1988.

Young, Stanley. *The Missions of California*. San Francisco: Chronicle Books, 1988.

ACKNOWLEDGMENTS

It is not only the heroines of Tennessee Williams who survive thanks to the kindness of strangers, nor only the Beatles who get along with the help of their friends. We all get along with the help of our friends, and a book of this sort, which wanders across many scholarly preserves, can only be written if strangers are willing to go beyond acquiescence to trespass and provide supplies and encouragement to the trespasser.

I think first of Bernard L. Fontana and James E. Ivey, who know the Southwest and who welcomed me. Both wrote commentary on my draft texts which took the form of expository essays often of greater value than the drafts themselves. Those essays, diffident offerings of comradeship in learning, worked their way into many of these pages. My old friend James P. Shannon offered detailed improvements to my efforts on matters of geography and theology. David Hurst Thomas and Lorann S. A. Pendleton not only wrote helpful suggestions but were cheerful guides to the terrain. No one can write about missions with any intelligence without relying upon the work of these scholars; to have the pleasure of knowing them as companions is a joy. David Noble of Santa Fe has written the best guidebook to the archaeology of that region, and he generously disclosed to my wife and me many of its wonders.

One of the grand experiences of my life was an expedition from San Diego northward to San Francisco, from mission to mission, with Ramon Gutierrez. Dave Warren, Rick West, Rina Swentzel, and Rayna Green saw to it that this work was no more Eurocentric than it is, and I thank Dave in particular for his counsel during a time in which he might easily have felt he had no time for other people's needs.

I rejoice in having had the ignition of George Kubler some years ago to undertake this study. Peggy Liss educated me about Spain and Mexico, and Judith Sandoval about the history of Mexican buildings. Lonn Taylor and Richard Ahlborn were among many people at the National Museum of American History who gave me ideas, information, and encouragement.

Matt Mulcahy assisted me in research, Joyce Ramey in the logistics of creation; Naomi Glass organized my life and kept other chores and importunities from overwhelming this process.

Frances Kennedy was companion and inspiration and co-conspirator throughout, once again.

David Larkin would like to thank David Yubeta of the National Park Service at Tumacácori for sharing his knowledge of adobe mission construction in southern Arizona and for getting the photographer and the designer into and onto the roofs of missions in Sonora. Thanks also to Ron Foreman of the Southwest Parks and Monuments Association in Tucson for the use of its material, to Lawrence Ormsby and Carol Thickstun for their drawings, and lastly, to the councils of the mission pueblos, who helped us take pictures with the minimum of disturbance to their congregations.

Opposite: A detail from the main portal of San Xavier del Bac.

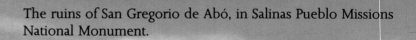

The ruins of San Gregorio de Abó, in Salinas Pueblo Missions National Monument.